TRANSFORM

INTO

LIGHTBODY

Cynthia D. Clayton, Ph.D.

Illustrations by Freydoon Rassouli

Visit Rassouli.com

© 2017

ISBN: 978-1-5136-0177-9

Oh God, place light in my heart, and light in my soul, light upon my tongue, light in my eyes and light in my ears, place light at my right, light at my left, light behind me and light before me, light above me and light beneath me. Place light in my nerves, and light in my flesh, light in my blood, light in my hair and light in my skin! Give me light, increase my light, make me light!

~ Zia Inayat Khan

LIGHTBODY THROUGH THE AGES

Superconductive Body— Indian Vedas

Diamond or Jade Body— Taoism

Diamond Body— Vajrayana

Adamantine Body— Tantra

Sacred Body, or Super Celestial Body— Sufism

'Wujud al-Aqdas', or *'Jism asli haqiqi'*— Sufism

Radiant Body— Neo-Platonism

Immortal Body— Hermeticism

Body of Bliss— Kriya Yoga

Perfect Body— Mithraism

Golden Body— Emerald Tablets

Holy Flesh— Catholicism

Glorified Body, or Resurrection Body—

Christianity

Rainbow Body or the Great Transfer—

Tibetan Buddhism

Devi and Devta— Brahma Kumaris

Spiritual Body— Christianity

Luminous Being— Egyptian

CALL OF FREEDOM by Rassouli

Contents

IN THE BEGINING by Russouli

Preface

It absolutely causes me to grin from ear to ear, when someone infers that the exploration of the light-body phenomena is New Age. There is no concept as ancient as the idea that we came from the Light and are returning to the Light. Yet, much of the world's population is foreign to the idea that... we ARE the light!

Current scientific research in Bio-photonics points to facts metaphysicians have known for thousands of years: that chi or prana is numinous light circulating in our electromagnetic body, and that our bodies are becoming vehicles for ascendant consciousness. My goal is to provide a new understanding of this inherent light-body.

The idea that the soul is on a journey toward actualization is supported by an enormous amount of literature describing ways to achieve our full human potential. But what happens *then*? What form does illumination take once a human being finally reaches the summit? A number of the world's great religions teach about the existence of an immortal light form to which all humans are heir. The seeds of this immortal essence are said to exist within each of us.

As a process, spiritual realization has progressive phases of emotional and mental transformation. However, I hope to bring awareness of tangible *physical* changes that occur as a person intensifies in consciousness through mystical or transcendent experiences. In the last stage of enlightenment, according to esoteric teachings of many religions and mystery schools, the human body itself is changed from flesh into light. Through the process of transubstantiation of the flesh, blood, skin, and bone, one actually becomes a being made of light. What at first seemed a baffling and mysterious subject became crystal clear by the end of my research. I present my findings here, which I hope will provide you with insight into this amazing and yet natural phenomena of the evolution of our species.

SHALL WE BEGIN?

TRANSCENDING LOVE by Rassouli

This genie is you

Chapter 1: Introduction

Like the Genie inside Aladdin's Lamp, a Magic Presence vibrates inside of us. It acts as our own personal transformer, assisting our transcendence into the next stage of human evolution. It can be called our soul essence, or our core frequency. Through the ages it has been referred to by many terms. (Preceding page) The belief that we are made of light and are evolving into light-bodies is in all religious traditions, mystery schools and esoteric texts. And, it has not only been considered possible for the human body to evolve into pure energy, into a Body of Light, proof actually exists of thousands of cases. This Light is not the physical light made of photons, but is of a higher frequency undetected by current scientific instruments. We raise our frequency and live in the more harmonious dimensions. A person in lightbody would be invisible to the average person.

There is no escape, it is inevitable, occurs organically, and *everyone* transforms- sooner or later. Transformation into lightbody is not optional! It can take hundreds of lifetimes, or much fewer. It is the final spiritual stage... the exit door. Arriving at the natural endgame of the human experience, we merge with our inherent divine nature, and what unfolds is the beginning of a new octave as our galactic selves. Although this may sound like science-fiction, remember, science-fiction is often the precursor for reality.

Humanity is now receiving this revelation, and we are here at this time to serve the world during the long-heralded Shift into the Golden Age of expanded consciousness. We finally understand the integration of the human and divine as the final evolutionary stage of human beings. When a soul is fully evolved it will develop from a Homo-Sapien into a "Homo-Universalis," then, become "Homo-Luminous." If you are reading this book, your soul has pre-ordained this time to summon the Light from within your body, like polishing Aladdin's lamp. You liberate your Light and release your true essence, transposing into the Eternal Self.

Do you recall the timeworn movie *Cocoon*? The ending demonstrated a swimming pool full of euphoric senior citizens transforming into their hidden light-bodies. It didn't look like a bad way to go, did it! Jungle guides suddenly emerge to rescue the main characters in the movie *The Celestine Prophecy*, then exit disappearing into a door of translucent light. They do this several times, secretly, but eventually are witnessed as beings of light. Ascended Masters throughout history have been spotted materializing and de-materializing, from Mother Mary to Babaji. This was long before the series Star Trek popularized the notion of releasing the physical elements of the body in a transporter. We fondly remember, "Beam me up, Scotty!"

So, how do we achieve the next stage? There is proof in the academic world that 160,000 enlightened masters in Tibet and China achieved their Rainbow Bodies.[2] And this is achievable today, as are even higher levels of lightbody such as The Great Transfer. This book you are reading right now is the key to your culmination... and to your freedom!

The process divulged in the practices herein, is to invoke and commune with Light, to hang out with the Light of our innate or primordial state of mind, pure Presence, and as the mind gains its freedom and becomes lucid and limitless... the elements in our bodies release their light. However, until we have peeled away all the masks of personality roles and discovered the pure Self within, and learned to be a *Bodhicitta* of unconditional love and service to others, we are not able to connect to our soul and the Light within for long enough periods to fully transform.

Let us investigate together. What is so fascinating about light that it captivated one of the most brilliant and curious minds on the planet? Albert Einstein enthusiastically revealed: "For the rest of my life, I will reflect on what light is."[3] Light within the human body is currently studied by a new branch of biology called Biophotonics, within the parent Institute of Biophysics (IIB) founded by Fritz-Albert Popp and his colleagues in 1996. There are now about 40 research groups worldwide.[4] Bio-photonics is measuring a fifth-circulatory system in the human body- of moving light. It makes sense that when actively accelerated this fifth-circulatory system enhances and regulates physical transformation.

Scientists have long been intrigued by this inner light, wondering why acupuncturists succeeded for thousands of years in their healing arts by tracking electromagnetic impulses inside meridians. This idea of light circulating in the body is not a recent New Age philosophy, but received interest by scientists even of the stature of Albert Einstein and Isaac Newton. As far back as 1717, Newton speculated: "Are not the gross bodies and light convertible into one another, and may not bodies receive much of their activity from the particles of light which enter their composition?"[5]

The idea of converting into a body of light always summons discussion of the processes of resurrection and ascension. A few thousand years ago, according to an esoteric book *The Essenes - Children of the Light,* Jesus talks to a group of friends during his youth as an Essene. The discussion portrays that he already knows about ascension.

In the first level of spiritual ascension, you continue in the physical body for a while. But when your task on earth is completed, you go forward into physical ascension. The physical body dissolves into light, and from then on as an ascended being you live within your body of light. Spirit and matter merge and become one, and the body is raised into a higher realm.[6]

Jewish and Christian doctrine hold that several Bible figures ascended. Enoch ascended, great-grandfather of Noah. "By faith Enoch was taken from this life, so that he did not experience death; he could not be found, because God had taken him away."[7] Jesus bodily ascended to heaven forty days after his resurrection. Elijah, Abraham, Moses, Isaiah, Ezra, and Mary also ascended.

My effort to explore and connect the resurrection/ascension theme across traditions is supported by research by Father Francis Tiso, a priest of the Diocese of Isernia-Venafro, Italy. He has traveled and studied the rainbow body extensively, and the spiritual path and practices that correspond to both the Christian Resurrection Body of Jesus and the Rainbow Body of Nyingma Buddhists. "The Rainbow Body shows the possibilities inherent in the human body, which seems to be a distillation apparatus into which all the energies of the universe flow in the direction of enlightenment."[8]

The purpose of a lightbody is to bring forth the spirit, the light, creating a union of spirit with matter. The

soul's nature fully manifests through the body. The body
becomes light and immortal when they are truly joined.

GREETING THE DAWN by Rassouli

There are many types of light: particulate (photonic), superluminal, even the light of consciousness. What is "numinous" light? According to Guruji Krishnananda, founder of the Light Channels and Light Age Masters groups in India: "This 'Light' is not the physical light. It exists at a subtler level as numinous energy, is everywhere, has intelligence and all the positive energies of love, peace, wisdom, and healing."[9]

Picture the infinite cosmos, the earth spinning along with other heavenly bodies in swirling, oscillating, vibrating energy. Numinous light is such energy. We swim in it and internalize it... like fish inhabiting water. We are connected to it as our Source Field.

This is exactly the vision of one of the most significant physicists of the twentieth century, David Bohm, in his groundbreaking work with electronic plasma. "Bohm proposed that creation was a living sea of electrons in perpetual dynamic flux, an unending sea of light, a "holomovement" in which matter is a crystallized form of light."[10] "Let there be light!" is not a figure of speech; everything is light, and our human bodies are crystallized light.

There at first appears to be a contradiction between Genesis 1:3, the first day of creation when God says, "Let there be light," and the fourth day of creation, when God created the sun, the moon, and the stars (Gen. 1:16-18). If God did not create the sun until the fourth day, it might be asked, what was the light of the first day? It was numinous primordial light, adamantine particles, the light of paradise.

There are many creation stories with light coming forth from the void. The Jewish Kabbalistic tradition has a beautiful sacred story about the origination of light, "The Shattering of the Vessels" (*Shevirat ha-kelim*).

...the light that came into being filled the darkness, and ten holy vessels came forth, each filled with primordial light. In this way God sent forth those ten vessels, like a fleet of ships, each carrying its cargo of light. Had they all arrived intact, the world would have been perfect. But the vessels were too fragile to contain such a powerful, divine light. They broke open, split asunder, and all the holy sparks were scattered like sand, like seeds, like stars.[11]

Those full of the Light of God, aware they are holy sparks, are gathering and joining across the planet. Light is attracting Light, and becoming the One Light that will indeed save the world from itself.

And when enough holy sparks have been gathered, the broken vessels will be restored, and Tikkun Olam, the repair of the world, awaited so long, will finally be complete. Therefore it should be the aim of everyone to raise these sparks from wherever they are imprisoned and to elevate them to holiness by the power of their soul.[12]

Numinous light is the *source* of all creation, and the *substance* of all creation, carrying all life force. Some other terms for this active principle forming any living thing are Prana (Vedic Sanskrit), Chi (Chinese), Mana (Hawaiian), Ki (Japanese), vital energy (Western), adamantine particles, the fifth element, God particles, pure consciousness, pre-creation Light sent from Light Realms, the building blocks of creation, manna from heaven, the existence in all things manifest, ether, love, life, intelligence, power, primal energy, Infinite Spirit, the Inner Light of God, life-energy, life-force, breath, air or gas, Holy Spirit, Shekinah, and Shakti (cosmic energy). Oh, and my favorite from Star Wars...The Force!

Prana and light are interchangeable terms in many traditions. Prana was first expounded in the Upanishads, as part of the worldly, physical realm, sustaining the body like mana. It is also considered the mother of thought- and thus, is also in the mind. Prana suffuses all living forms as the essence of life (or spirit), but is not itself the soul. Prana has been most recognized in traditional and alternative Eastern medicine, martial arts, philosophy and spirituality.

Many authors I researched from India use the word "Light" like those in the West use the word "God." This Light is an omnipresent, omniscient, omnipotent Presence. I simply call this mysterious, magical essence "Light" in my discourse presented in this book, and it manifests both outwardly and inwardly, above and below, and is the living, vibrating Magic Presence within our lamps, the "Genie" waiting to be freed.

Most religious and spiritual traditions believe we came from Light and are returning to the Light. Jesus said, in the Gospel of Thomas, "If they say to you, 'Where did you come from?' say to them, 'We came from the light, the place where the light came into being on its own accord and established itself and became manifest..."[13]

However, what I hope to transmit to you more than anything else in this book, please, is get past *we came from the light and are returning to the light*, which is only half the story. WE ARE THE LIGHT!

The Taoist view on lightbody is both mystical and practical. Lee Holden reminds us light is actually in the very fiber of our cells. We are eating light in whatever form of food it created that we choose. We receive light through breathing, as the Chi energy attached to air molecules. Light is in water, too, as the source of energy behind the cycle of evaporation. We consume light, and then it literally manifests as our body, and becomes our nervous system, our thoughts, our glands, and our metabolism. "We are light-driven beings!"[14] All atomic particles are fundamentally complex photons. (LIGHT) These ever-present effervescent photons are simply what you might think of as the creative impulse.

Taoism stresses alchemy in development of the lightbody, or Golden Body. An understanding of the elements and energy have been taught for thousands of years as practical tools rather than religious thought. Within your body you can alchemically change negative energy into positive energy, and transform un-useful energy into useful energy. As the frequency of the body raises through internal alchemy- burning up, transmuting and releasing all that does not serve our higher good- our physical energy transforms into a more subtle energy of light and levity. The goal is to let go of what covers up our true self. "Our natural state is to glow."[15]

Understanding our energy bodies offers us a deep connection to life, useful for spiritual growth and physical, mental and emotional health. By increasing our Light quotient through internal alchemy we influence our emotions, our mental bodies, and our spiritual bodies. We can lighten our physical body from toxins and excesses, we can brighten our emotional body with more light-heartedness and joyfulness, dealing with our emotions and loving more. We can brighten our mental body with great thoughts, intuition, and clarity. The vibration of illumination in our minds rises up and creates illumination in our spirits. We lighten our etheric body by releasing the weight of our past- with forgiveness.

There is an emerging interest in "cleaning house," and many modalities to do so are emerging in energy medicine, acupuncture, acupressure, Reiki, Tai-Chi, Chi-Gong, ultra-violet light purification, and chakra clearing, to name a few.

Elevating prana to a holy substance that is consumable and absorbable explains how thousands of people on the planet called "breatharians" do not eat or even drink, but live on prana at times. Perhaps it will be possible in the future to harness nourishment in this manner. When we do not have dense physical bodies but live in our light-bodies, we will only eat or drink for pleasure. Don't worry; we won't have to give up chocolate!

The "Story of Light" continues, and we know we are an intimate part of that progression. One cannot define numinous light any easier than defining God. But in chapter 4, we examine the findings and implications of scientific research. Ultimately, it is about lifting up our consciousness into absolute consciousness. Our mindfulness and expression of the Light is mastery, and by aligning with it we rise in awareness and harmonic vibration. We create a more compassionate world, Eden re-instated, and prepare for the next part of the Journey.

Light is the secret catalyst, added to the ingredients inside the lamp, to produce the sacred combustion...

14

WAYS TO THE RAINBOW by Rassouli

Chapter 3: The Soul's Journey

The transformation of enlightened beings rising into a New Age involves several factors, many of which are cosmological and will not be discussed here, and all of them are coming together now, giving us the opportunity to make a big evolutionary leap. The next leap in the evolution of the physical body will transform it in such a way, that once this transformation is complete, our present physical bodies become light bodies. Sri Aurobindo, a great Indian teacher and mystic, stated that "divine body" is the ultimate stage of human evolution. He felt that a deathless condition resulting from transubstantiation of the fleshly body could be attained by personal effort, meditation, and divine grace.

The lightbody is basically the core of our being, unmanifested until certain triggers release its development; it is the return vehicle of our soul to go Home. Human souls are intelligent, conscious beings composed of subtle energy not detected by today's scientific devices. Descended from realms very different than this physical universe, we are living here temporarily in the gross form of physical bodies. We are visitors come to earth to experience life and creativity. In the descent of the soul we lost our feeling of connection to Source. In our ascending state toward spiritual perfection and dominion, we regain that connection, and continue our experience here in total awareness with Source. Our souls are trying to fully embody, and step into their full divinity. Once we have a lightbody, the soul can manifest its original glory through it. This was God's plan all along, for God is the holder of all souls.

The soul's need is to express itself on the physical plane, fully and without limitations. Souls live in human bodies and experience life here, yet the capacity of the soul is far greater than the capacity of our current bodies on this planet. So our bodies must transform. The experience of a soul's return to lightbody is the destiny of being human.

The soul is a speck of light, and is immortal. When the soul's nature fully manifests through the physical body, the body becomes Light and immortal. This is the union of Matter and Spirit, when the Light body is able to bring forth the Spirit (Light). This is the purpose of a Light body.[16]

When the physical body evolves to its highest state, its frequency reaches such a level that it becomes a very subtle light body that is free of all biological processes like breathing, digestion, circulation, aging and death.

During the transformation of the physical body into a Lightbody, the mind and intellect become pure and carry more and more light. With this they become free of negative thoughts and emotions. The intellect will carry higher thoughts; the mind will produce higher emotions. And even the vital body carries higher product in its channels. With regular meditation, light channeling and experiencing light, the body, the mind and the intellect carry more and more light and become light, ultimately.[17]

Our souls are covered with various layers of "bodies," often called physical, etheric, emotional, mental and spiritual bodies. In the *Vedas* (the wisdom and knowledge of the ancient Rishis of India) these coverings are called five Koshas, "sheaths," or consciousness vehicles- the physical, the vital life-force, the mental, the intelligence, and the bliss sheaths. These vehicles referred to in the Vedic tradition include the Anamaya Kosha, or "electromagnetic body" and the Pranamaya Kosha, or "epikinetic body" of vibratory harmonics.

Rupert Sheldrake referred to these as morphic fields, or "non-material regions of influence." Another model is the Multi-Bodied Transduction Model (MBTM) of J.J. Hurtak and Bruce Curtis, that can make sense of the human being as a complex of interpenetrating consciousness, energy fields and vibratory bodies.[18]

One may participate with the five Koshas or consciousness vehicles that together function as a life/light continuum. Creating a Merkabah connects humankind to more subtle realms of existence, more advanced consciousness time zones. We must cleanse and raise the vibration in each layer or body in order to allow our lightbody to emerge. By our communing with and channeling Light we organically disperse into it. As we clean up our sheaths or bodies surrounding our inner Light, it shines forth... and we become transparent.

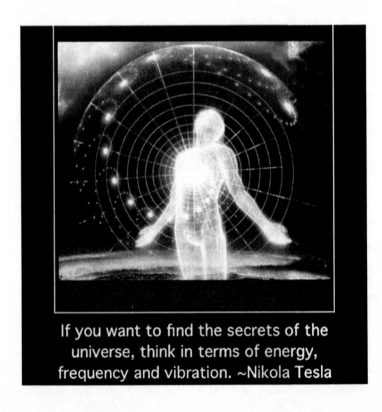

If you want to find the secrets of the universe, think in terms of energy, frequency and vibration. ~Nikola Tesla

Everything Is Energy

Although we identify ourselves with our physical body, we are actually energy or light beings.. Every thought, word, feeling and thing is energy....everything! Things that appear to be solid are actually very tightly compacted energy particles creating a shape, form or physical matter. Our physical body, that part of us that is not eternal, is surrounded by our eternal divine essence consisting of our emotional, mental and spiritual energetic layers. We are much more than our physical body; we are actually multidimensional, energetic, spiritual beings having a physical human experience. It is important for us to bring into our awareness the many layers of our energetic body. This is the key to our self-empowerment. When it is brought into our awareness, our soul will begin to integrate all of the layers of ourselves bringing us into a state of wholeness. Each of us needs to become aware of who we really are and connect with all of our energy.

Nobel laureate Dr. Albert Szent-Györgi, father of modern biochemistry, stated: "The cell is a machine driven by energy. It can thus be approached by studying matter or by studying energy."[19] Until recently, the human body has most often been examined as a contained system of cells outside the greater matrix of energy and consciousness. Yet, quantum physicists demonstrate that we are energetic receivers and transmitters, connected to a wider field. I have no doubt that continued research in astrophysics and quantum physics will support Bohm's holographic universe theory, with greater proof that our body/ mind/ spirit vehicles are connected to a greater whole. New studies show that consciousness is at work beyond cellular and molecular levels, and may guide us to understanding.

We are beginning to map some type of light circulatory system operating on an energetic level in a markedly different manner from that of its molecular counterparts. ... an entire body distinct from the chemical body that interpenetrates it. Such a body has been termed the electromagnetic body and may be a vehicle of consciousness projection.[20]

The study of our electromagnetic field has largely been its radiation extending outside our body. Research at HeartMath has demonstrated a radiant field coming from the heart region, easily recorded fifteen feet away. The idea of auras is not new; several saints and masters were seen with a halo or light around them. And, have you ever walked into a room where you interrupted an argument, and the air was so thick you could cut it with a knife? Our emotions and thoughts are clearly projected, demonstrated in Dr. Emoto's experiments with water, and extended when Bruce Lipton proposes our projected consciousness interacts with reality; therefore, it's almost impossible to be objective in research situations.

"Electromagnetic Body" describes an enhanced view that our physical body receives, utilizes and radiates light. "... consider that the human body functions at some levels as a quasi-"light" body, transducing signals locally and non-locally, both from within itself and from extra-biologic sources."[21]

Bio-Computer/Bio-Photonics

Evidence of a hyper-fast communication system in the body seems to indicate that the human body works as a "bio-computer", operating on many levels of information simultaneously, interpenetrated and surrounded by fields of consciousness. Research by the University of California at Irvine, "...has demonstrated the transmission of information at speeds of *several orders of magnitude* greater than nerve impulses."[22] "While it may not be at quite the velocity of an e-m pulse, it is more than 2-orders of magnitude faster than the nervous system."[23]

In the '70's, German scientist Fritz-Albert Popp discovered that the human body emits light. Bio-photons are weak light emitted within the cells of our bodies. The role of the bio-photon is multifaceted, but much data confirms that bio-photons transmit information, as mediators of intercellular communication.

> All living organisms, including humans, emit a
> low intensity glow that cannot be seen by the
> naked eye, but can be measured by
> photomultipliers that amplify the weak signals
> several million times and enable the researchers
> to register it in the form of a diagram. As long as
> they live, cells and whole organisms give off a
> pulsating glow with a mean intensity of several
> up to a few ten thousand photons per second
> and square centimeter.[24]

Popp's research is the focus of the International Institute of Biophysics (IIB) founded by Popp and his colleagues in 1996, now an international research network "...at universities in the USA, China, Russia, Poland, India, Japan, Korea, Israel, Italy, England, and Germany. Altogether, there are about 40 bio-photon research labs."[25]

"Junk" DNA

I predict major breakthroughs in forthcoming DNA research will hold some keys on lightbody. Much research is being conducted on "Junk DNA," the 97% of DNA with unknown function. What undiscovered codes may exist in this unused DNA to release human blue-print information? Is it potential programming receptors waiting for our axia-tonal system to come online, assisting our physical transformation into Light? A lot of controversy exists.

In the fall of 2012, 30 research papers decreed that they had discovered the purpose of Junk DNA.

... 30 research papers, including six
in *Nature* and additional papers published
online by *Science*, sound the death knell for the
idea that our DNA is mostly littered with useless
bases. A decade-long project, the Encyclopedia
of DNA Elements (ENCODE), has found that
80% of the human genome serves some purpose,
biochemically speaking.[26]

But immediately, other scientists counteracted. Sean Addy, a bio informatics expert who runs a lab at the Howard Hughes Medical Institute, was one of the many scientists who spoke out against the Encode misinterpretation of their own results. He says there is still mostly "junk" or undisclosed DNA in our bodies.[27] So the verdict is still out on what percent is dormant. Even 20 percent would make one wonder, why?

The Source of Consciousness

Another controversy holds more promise of finding common ground. Remember the riddle, *which came first, the chicken or the egg?* There is a new understanding of the interplay of consciousness and energy within our bodies. Consciousness does not grow from and emit from the body, it is not reducible to information fields emerging *from* a certain stage of complex material. Nobel Prize winner and originator of the Quantum Theory, Max Planck, said: "I regard consciousness as fundamental. I regard matter as a derivative of consciousness."[28]

This is also the ancient view of masters from India. Consciousness is first, matter is created from that.

Consciousness is in everything, a force moving between our minds and all things, and all things are alive with energy and light that we are learning to direct through focus, intention, and conscious creation, as exhibited in Lipton's and Emoto's work.

Hurtak perceives matter and energy

... as complementary aspects of information
fields that emerge from consciousness, which is
the source and ground of all that appears. As the
universal and ubiquitous presence,
consciousness is the hidden variable in the
cosmos that in varying degrees directs and
participates in all quantum events. In sum, it is
the core reality holding the entire multi-
dimensional universe together in its unified
field.[29]

Reviving the Universal Grid

Have you ever heard of "Astro-Acupuncture"? All this speculation on linking our consciousness and body to a greater grid of energy- is not new. Perhaps we are coming full circle in our knowledge. The *Nei Jing*, one of the most important classics of Taoism, as well as the highest authority on traditional Chinese medicine, incorporated an acupuncture system that was once viewed as extending beyond the limits of the human body and into the greater cosmos. It is beginning to appear that humankind is working only with a truncated version of acupuncture when compared with the ancient practice.

The newest translations of the *Nei Jing* confirm this more expanded model of acupuncture science.[30] This extended system could be called an axia-tonal system of vibratory communication, by virtue of its functioning through meridians with diverse fields of light and sound.[31]

Vedic sages were also schooled in an analogous science known as Jyotish dating back five-thousand years ago in India. "Jyoti" is light and "isha" is lord, so it translates into "The Lord of Light" or "The Knowledge of Light." Vedic scripture describes Jyotish as the "Eye of the Vedas," or the Light which illumines the universal knowledge encapsulated in the Vedas. This most likely was the oldest known cosmic divination of astronomy and astrology from which Babylonian, Egyptian, Greek, Roman and modern Western Astrology diverged.

It is easy to see how we fast forward thousands of years, but continue to view our connection to a grid or matrix of light around the earth. We feel connected to this by an internal compass, and equally to the universal guidance system it offers us.

EXALTATION by Rassouli

JOY OF UNION by Rassouli

FOUNTAIN OF GRACE by Rassouli

Chapter 5:
Understanding Frequencies and the Tone of Your Soul

All matter is moving at different speeds, and usually converts into other more or less active forms of energy— water to steam or ice, for instance. So what might I convert into? LIGHTBODY! We are luminous, energetic, creative beings moving into our authentic Selves.

The evolutionary phases of progressing into lightbody can be understood as "rising in frequency." The terms "frequency" and "vibration" are often used interchangeably outside the physics classroom, especially in regards to electromagnetic energy when discussed in metaphysics. For the purpose of understanding the fundamental causes, nature and relations of things, I simply use "frequency", though more correct would be "vibrational frequency" or "frequency of vibration". I personally see frequency as a maintained state and vibration as the oscillating to arrive at that state.

George Gurdjieff's "Atomism" supports the notion that as we increase in frequency we lose density, and become light. While it did not hold up to newer science, it has merit in offering "worlds" of light, planes of existence at different octaves. In Atomism, vibrating matter is in everything- the world, things, the void, the entire psychic, intellectual, emotional, volitional, and other inner processes. He states:

> Absolute can be called world 1, whose atoms
> alone are really 'indivisible.' In the Absolute,
> vibrations are the most rapid and matter is the
> least dense. In the next world, vibrations are
> slower and matter denser; and further on matter

is still more dense and vibrations [would be] correspondingly slower.[32]

The Absolute would be the octave of the Body of Light.

We are in a process of becoming high-frequency beings, of changing from a relatively dense body and personality into nothing less than our souls... fully saturated in time, space, and matter. We're starting to see life as energy and awareness. Our inner world is alive, and we may be ultrasensitive, often feeling a quickening in our bodies. Ultimately, we are designed to effectively raise our vibration into a higher dimension where spirit and matter merge- without having to die to do it.

The concept of frequency offers a clear understanding of changes occurring in our electromagnetic bodies. You can monitor and change your frequency to rapid and less dense states by adjusting conditions in the body, emotions and thoughts. Your vibration is generated from inside you by your own choices of how you react to life. Your energy state is a blend of the contracted and expanded frequencies of your body, emotions, and thoughts at any given moment. Although affected by other people's vibrations and the vibrations of the world, how you want to feel is basically- your choice. The higher your vibration the more light you hold, the faster your light particles vibrate, the higher your consciousness and the stronger you are connected to your soul and Godself.

When your vibration is low, your light particles are vibrating slowly and become condensed. Your energy literally feels heavy because you are not in alignment with your soul or divine self and are mostly operating from your lower self or ego of distorted beliefs. Fear, anger, resentment, blame, guilt, jealousy, judgment, shame, addiction, being unforgiving, conditional love, lack of self-worth, greed, separation consciousness and poor health keep you in very dense low vibrating energy.

When you are a high vibrational being you recognize your divinity and the divinity within others. You are in alignment with your soul, which is nourished by spirit; you are vibrantly healthy and your life flows with ease and grace. This is your "home frequency", the vibration of your soul as it expresses through your body. It is called *home* because it conveys an experience that's as close to heaven on earth as you can get. To evolve into your lightbody you must find and remain as much as possible in your home frequency, your soul's eternal indestructible tone. Finding this is really the big turning point in your transformation process. Imagine that your home frequency is reprogramming and retraining your cells, because it is. Feel it!

What are the keys to finding home frequency? The more you allow your soul to shine through you... the higher your personal vibration will be. As you allow your soul to take charge of your life, you vibrate with your soul's true higher purpose and divine blueprint, and eventually rise into a Body of Light, a new dimension where spirit and matter merge.[33] You can discover and uncover your soul and shine out any time you want!

How does home frequency feel?

... a resonance that conveys your soul's love, truth, abundance, and joy. It bubbles up from your tiny "quantum entities," waving out   through your cells and tissues to fill the space   around you. ...the kind of gorgeous, bright frequency that babies radiate.[34]

You can also tell immediately when you leave that level... usually you've accepted fears or doubts in your mind, or became overrun with increased desires, emotional or mental clutter. But the natural vibration of your soul is underneath, always there, and acts as a compass to bring you back in attunement. Then, the naturally high-frequency energy stabilizes your life which unfolds with luck, meaning, and joy.

We are responsible to go within and re-calibrate to our home frequency, so we may align with our soul's true higher purpose and divine blueprint. This return to balance and harmony is the time you want to ask your Higher Self questions, or envision your life. The best ideas and answers come out of your home frequency, which is similar to Ester Hicks' (Abraham) vortex of creation. To stay in the vortex when you're in an unfamiliar context, it's important to remember who you are. You are a limitless being made of consciousness, light and energy, connected to the All-That-Is through a unified field that coordinates and regulates the flow of creation perfectly. And your basic substance... is Light!

We have the potential to raise our vibration to such a point that the layers of our being (our energetic bodies) unify and together activate the creation of our lightbody. When this occurs, we have reached a very high vibrational state where our spiritual Self or Godself is able to merge with our physical body. This cannot occur until we have raised our vibration high enough for divine union to occur. This is the moment of enlightenment and the return to one's true spiritual essence and identity.

We will see in Chapter 8: Stages of Lightbody, how the rising and falling terrain of frequency shifting affects us. You may think you are losing your mind, and fortunately you are, in a manner. This evolutionary shift takes you up and down like a roller coaster, going in and out of each stage many times until you find equilibrium. You are gradually becoming more aware, sensitive, visionary, empathic, and loving. Hence, the biggest challenge of the next few years will be working with your sensitivity, keeping your personal vibration clear, and learning to use "frequency principles" to live through the coming times.

I AM the Violet
Flame In action in
me now
I AM the Violet
Flame To light
alone I bow
I AM the Violet Flame
In mighty cosmic
power I AM the Light
of God Shining every
hour
I AM the Violet
Flame Blazing like a
sun
I AM God's sacred
power Freeing
everyone.

St. Germaine's Violet Flame Gift

PROCESSION OF THE LIGHT WORKERS by Rassouli

Chapter 6: Ascended Masters

Students of metaphysics and consciousness ask: *what is the innermost nature of the mind, and how is consciousness evolving?* I promote that when our mind reaches and accepts the clear-light of Infinite Mind, nirvana, samadhi, Christ-consciousness, Buddha-mind, cosmic consciousness, and so forth, we naturally reach higher planes of our inner Godself and become a Body of Light. All of the Masters achieved clear-light mind, learned to live in non-judgmental awareness of the moment, offered unconditional love, and were free from control by the ego. Your energy bodies (physical, mental, emotional, etheric) must align to the truth of your inner perfection, with your heart the key. The more you love unconditionally your luminosity increases, and you radiate into your diamond lightbody.

The idea I would MOST like you to hear in this entire book? Become aware of what you already are! You are a magnificent being, with all the components to make this transition built-in and ready to go.

For, whatever the human mind will ever be, it
already is. ... Whatever you will become, you
already are, because it is already in your mind
and you don't have to add anything outwardly to
yourself, but merely become aware of what you
already are."35

The seeds of immortality are said to exist within each of us, planted since souls' creation and purpose to achieve spiritual mastery. Like the Genie in our magic lamp!

All religions believe in ascension into a different dimension or heavenly plane, and have "ascended masters." Devotees pray to them, invoke their presence, develop relationships, and ask for assistance or guidance. Buddhists call on one of the ascended Buddhas, Muslims invoke Muhammad, Christians appeal to Jesus or Mother Mary, Hindus have many Masters they request- Krishna, Shiva, Durga, and so forth. Someone wanting to compose a symphony may try connecting with a master like Mozart. All masters who have passed on before us, known and unknown, have ascended. They earned the privilege of leaving the life-death cycle, the illusion of separation from the Oneness called God. They continue to exist energetically in an ascended state of high-frequency light-bodies, serving those who call on them.

They are often seen in a "descended" state by devotees in visitations. There are Ascended Masters who have been sighted and rumored to appear and disappear throughout time in various guises: Mary Magdalene, Jesus, Mother Mary, Sai Baba, Saint Germain, Kuthumi, El Morya, Sanat Kumara, the list goes on and on. The most famous example of a Master living in a lightbody is Majavatar Babaji, seen by many in the Himalayas of India. Also, legend has it, that many beings live in Shambhala for thousands of years in light bodies. If masters wish to "descend" from higher vibrating realms they can re-embody, calling in the elements needed for earth-plane existence. But it is draining on them to stay in this density for long, and most of their work is done from a higher plane.

It may seem a big stretch from our current everyday mindset, yet reality will shift when we realize just how unlimited we are.

Perhaps, as many of us become enlightened or self-realized—what I am terming transparent or made completely of diamond light (becoming lightbodies) —we'll discover we have the ability to ascend and descend through the realms, taking our physical bodies with us if we want.

As we thoroughly grasp the principles in
materializing and dematerializing within
physical reality, it may not be much of a stretch
at all to "ascend".[36]

Eventually, the Masters' bodies of light may merge into the Oneness, in union with All-That-Is, or head off to other cosmic missions. Then, the current earth-plane students ready to accept their white robes of spiritual perfection will ascend, and become the next level of ascended masters. Are YOU ready for this? My main purpose here is to tell you that when you are capable, the scepter will be passed to you. You must be ready to graduate to living a selfless life for others, prepared to guide souls in spiritual processes.

There are many other ways to serve, as well, such as earth angels, living teacher-masters, or cosmic travelers like the Melchizedek Order. Jesus suggested we can live in two worlds, the manmade and the heavenly plane. We can ascend more every day into the "heavenly" realm while living right here on earth. This kingdom already exists within us. It is a kingdom of Light...our connection to our infinite, eternal nature.

Where *are* the Beloved Masters like Buddha, Krishna, Jesus and Mary? Are they in the legendary Shambhala? Cloistered within etheric temples inside mountains? At Buddhist Pure Lands? Or, in some other dimension? They are closer than you think! In *The Celestine Prophecy*, the guides emerged from and re-entered a door of light, much like the ascended masters throughout history have done. The message is: ascended masters even arrive on the scene and assist us by driving jeeps while wearing blue jeans!

Today, with notable scientists like Stephen Hawking proposing alternate dimensions in their popular books, (he used eleven) [37], the notion of multiple dimensions is widely accepted. Discussions of the third through the seventh dimensions are common today in many circles. What would it be like to live in those dimensions, and what are the qualities and qualifications? Many feel light-workers live mostly in the fifth-dimension, while the Ascended Masters are in the seventh. Even Carl Sagan did a YouTube video on the fourth-dimension.[38] There are also Universal Studio Theme Parks around the world offering fourth-dimensional rides such as Sesame Street 4D© and Shrek 4D©.

So the idea of being connected to a much bigger picture beyond our limited picture seems totally plausible. A lot more is going on in many realms then we can possibly imagine! Man would be arrogant to think he knew everything, and indeed, scientists are still humble enough to call their ideas "theories."

BRINGER OF THE DAWN by Rassouli

Chapter 7: A Buddhist Path to Lightbody

Perhaps the most widely acclaimed instances of lightbody phenomenon are "Rainbow Bodies." This is the area of my research I found most intriguing, with an enormous amount of eyewitness accounts and extremely ardent practitioners. Adherents believe their teachings are the fastest and most powerful methods within all of Buddhism, and may lead to complete enlightenment in a single lifetime.

The indigenous Tibetan Bon and the Nyingma school of Tibetan Buddhism developed an emphasis to achieve liberation of the mind called Dzogchen. Also referred to as "Great Perfection" or Ati-yoga, its aim is attaining and maintaining the natural, primordial state of mind. The Nyingma is the oldest of the four Tibetan Buddhist orders, and is considered by many the fast-track to enlightenment. At death, supremely actualized Dzogchen masters are able to manifest rainbow bodies or even the highest form of lightbody- The Great Transfer. The rainbow body is the demonstration of the highest spiritual goal in Buddhism, the attainment of Buddhahood.

It was recorded that the first Master of the Dzogchen, Prahevajra (Garab Dorje), became like a ray of sunlight, then dissolved into space. While he was alive, many hundreds of thousands of his students attained rainbow body. Kathok Monastery in Tibet was called Kathok Dorje Den; 100,000 yogis have achieved rainbow body there.[39]

Even in recent years there have been a number of Tibetan Lamas, both Buddhist and Bon-po, who attained realization of the Rainbow Body at the end of their lives. In this century, Dud'jom Lingpa had thirteen students who attained rainbow body by following his lineage. Additionally, there are thousands of documented cases of human beings disappearing into light, recorded by the Chinese officials who invaded Tibet. Today, there are literally hundreds of priests and masters in India and Tibet utilizing these techniques to attain supreme realization and release.

Khenpo A-chos, a Tibetan monk, died amidst peculiar circumstances in 1998. The inquisitive Father Francis Tiso journeyed to Tibet to interview eyewitnesses. Lama A-chos and others had watched their friend's body shrink and disappear after seven days. Khenpo A-chos was regarded as a remarkable man, a highly evolved individual who was the embodiment of compassion and love. "He had the ability to teach even the roughest and toughest of types how to be a little gentler, a little more mindful. To be in the man's presence changed people."[40]

Inspired by the recent activity of lightbody phenomenon, David Steindl-Rast, a Benedictine monk and acquaintance of Tiso, was compelled to begin research on this supranormal activity. He gathered support from the Institute of Noetic Sciences (IONS) and The Esalen Institute.

He remarked in an interview that there are two main poles of Christian perspective on resurrection and ascension. Those that think the act of rising from the dead is only something Jesus could do, and not happen to anyone else. And those that feel Jesus lives on in spirit, and the resurrection had little to do with his body. However, he said, "A large number of people are open to the concept that the body, too, is significant in the spiritual realm, and that certain spiritual experiences are universal."[41]

He added:

> If we can establish as an anthropological fact
> that what is described in the resurrection of
> Jesus has not only happened to others, but is
> happening today, it would put our view of
> human potential in a completely different
> light.[42]

In arriving at the threshold of rainbow body, the inherent nature of the primordial state must be achieved for manifesting light. The light then manifests as five colors, the essences of the elements. (The essences of the elements interact to produce the elements themselves.) "When the Dzogchen adept realizes the unbounded nature of mind, he becomes able to transcend physicality and manifest the rainbow body."[43] Rather than "transcending physicality," a more accurate concept might be that the enlightenment expressed through rainbow bodies includes the body, minus the entire "residue" associated with samsaric existence. That is so thoroughly extinguished that no remainder whatsoever is left behind.

Their corpses shrink and mutate into lights, rays, and luminous spheres, while The Tibetan Book of the Dead may be read to the "dying," and rainbows are seen overhead. "It is as if the physical body, its material substances having been absorbed into its luminous essence, continues to live on as an aggregation of the elements in their subtle aspect."[44]

Liberation of Primordial Mind

Dzogchen teachings are not a school or system of philosophy, but a view of reality based on understanding the innate, luminous nature of mind. Followers try to recognize and maintain awareness of this abiding mode of one's mind. The state of the unbound nature of being

40

must be obtained in order to reach Buddhahood and release Rainbow Body at the end of life.

This primordial state is beyond all limits of time,
words and concepts, beyond creation and destruction;
it's the pure base of all existence. The principal Dzogchen
practice is to enter non-dual contemplation and to remain and deepen until one reaches total realization of
the natural condition. Non-dual contemplation is the
state of absolute presence; the awareness of luminosity,
the experience of clear light, the ability to manifest light.
As the mind gains its freedom and becomes limitless...
the elements release their light in a rainbow of colors.
The Rainbow Body! Often, bits of hair and fingernails are
left behind.

How does one achieve this state? In non-dual mind,
when held for an extended period, thoughts "self-
liberate." You are neither attached to nor rejecting
thoughts. As thoughts arise, one is not conditioned by
them. "...since the primordial state is inherently self-
liberating, by simply leaving thought alone, it liberates of
itself."45

During the meditation periods of simply sitting in
presence, there is no struggle. There is no feeling of being at war. It is simply a call to Light. The Light, knowing
neither resistance nor interference, just moves in, dissolving everything unlike Itself. This is what is meant by
self-liberating. Your Higher Self must keep reminding
your outer intellect which charges up your emotional
body, that in the changes occurring there need be no battle. Light is Self-luminous, intelligent substance,
connected to the infinite power of the universe; what
could one possibly have to fear or doubt?

Once practitioners have attained ultimate insight,
wisdom and compassion, they enter a phase in which
pure and total Presence is stabilized, through the practice of *Tregchod*.

Tregchod, which literally means '(spontaneous) cutting of tension', in the sense that as soon as the primordial state manifests and dualism is thus overcome, one instantly falls into a state of total relaxation, like a bundle of sticks, that, having been tightly bound together, falls loosely into a totally relaxed pattern as soon as the string binding it has been cut."[46]

What is released is the whole of conceptual thought, all one's tensions and rigidities, all mental obscurations which keep your Light of primordial awareness from shining through. This practice is a dissolving of the film or veil blocking us from our true nature, from seeing through all appearances. The result is resting in the luminous nature of Mind, becoming transparent.

Tregchod is mastering meditation in the state of union with the divine. The physical body is calmed to a death like state of samadhi, where one is able to consciously contemplate while in a deep state of union. *One achieves liberation into the primordial purity during this state, but there is no manifestation of lightbody until Thodgal is practiced.*

Once Tregchod is achieved and maintained, practitioners are then allowed to apply Thodgal...the secret teachings. They are so secret you aren't even allowed to purchase books anywhere on Thodgal practices unless you are a student of that level. I tried! Whereas Tregchod is focused on relaxation, cutting through and "the cessation of elements," Thodgal (literally meaning direct approach) is focused on action, "leaping over," and "the exhaustion of elements." Thodgal is the final practice of Dzogchen, dissolving the body into the essence of the elements at the time of death.

Once again, the cessation or dissolution of the elements in the instant of attaining liberation into primordial purity is Tregchod. Thodgal, the exhaustion of the elements "by perfecting the spontaneous accomplishment" is similar; they both purify the internal and external gross elements. But Thodgal leads to lightbody.

I feel that Grace has a lot to do with this process. That it is a state of God-realization in which divinity descends and transforms the spiritual, intellectual, mental, vital, and physical bodies into the highest perfection-physical immortality or God actualization. The human dualistic, afflicted emotional mind is exhausted into non-dualistic wisdom; you become the Koan. Simultaneously, the gross elemental body is exhausted into the Rainbow Body.

The Great Transfer

There is a difference between rainbow body and the Great Transfer. Great Transfer masters disappear without any trace, taking their bodies with them. This is similar to the ascension concept. The elements of the body are released into their original and indwelling essence of ether and light.

The realizations of the Great Transfer and the
Body of Light (rainbow body) are one and the
same; the only difference is that those who
attain the Great Transfer *do not have to go
through death in the clinical sense* in order to
move from manifestation in the material plane
to manifestation in the plane of the essence of
elements.[47]

The final result of Thodgal is complete union with the essence of all, a shift to cosmic awareness and connection. Living spiritual masters have dissolved their physical bodies into pure energy. Most followed secret, esoteric practices that had to be applied over a period of years, like Thodgal. These techniques resulted in the total transfiguration of the physical form into a form of self-sustaining light energy, immortal and indestructible, a condition that is permanent.

The Great Transfer represents a complete and radical transformation of one's status of being, a rediscovery of what was primordially present. "One liberates into this state of primordial purity, which is like space dissolving into space, or like clouds dissipating in the sky."[48] At this point, the contents of the physical body are exhausted and transformed into a Body of Light.

A practitioner's body becomes subtle and does not die, but while still living gradually becomes invisible to those who have normal karmic vision. Eventually, they disappear, the sign of the awakening in Buddhahood. "These beings remain in a satellite body form for as long as there is a service to perform for the benefit of ordinary beings. The Great Transfer confers great mystical and physical power to the Master for the benefit of others."[49] They communicate with individuals who embody necessary visionary clarity to engage with them. As our souls ripen and we approach fruition, so does the possibility of direct magical engagements with beings of Light.

Some known figures who have entered the stage of The Great Transfer are: Surativajra (Prahevajra), Manjushrimitra, Srisimha, Jnanasitra, Vimilamitra, Milarepa, and Padmasambhava.

44

Chaitanya Mahaprabhu (did not complete the process but was well on its way)

You only begin this final ascent into your divine nature and highest potential after many lifetimes of spiritual work. However, with a lot of clearing, healing, unconditional love, forgiveness, and Grace, many humans are making amazing progress in this lifetime. And as mentioned in the preceding chapter, the Dzogchen believe if the practitioner is sincere enough and free of ego and attachments, and maintains the purity of mind that is our natural state of luminosity, he can reach lightbody in this lifetime.

There are different levels of lightbody, and our energy bodies fluctuate back and forth between them, even on a daily basis. It's useful to know that symptoms of lightbody development you experience are not psychotic episodes or undiagnosed illness, but perfectly normal at a particular stage. Our physical bodies undergo remarkable changes in the final stages, and we withdraw to secrecy, like the caterpillar knowing it is birthing something beautiful.

These physical, mental and emotional difficulties are often called "ascension symptoms," since consciousness is expanding in a direction we consider higher. As we increase in frequency and lose density, this process has amazing shifts in perception and experiences of reality. Some people may ascend in consciousness through most of these stages organically, without experiencing any of the following conditions. Every individual is different, and some souls are capable of facilitating these stages in the subconscious or dream states.

There are mandatory phases of physical mutation to becoming a Body of Light. We have already discussed the empty DNA receptors waiting for a trigger. Lightbody is measured by the ability of your cells to metabolize light, to absorb ATP in the cells. One of the first steps in this process is for your Higher Self to instruct your cells to recognize and utilize all types of light as a new energy source. Then, prana feeds into every cell, not merely bathing the outer physical body in light. Your brain chemistry begins to change with more light, producing new synapses. And an intense sensory awakening occurs as a fifth-dimensional axial circulatory system begins to form and come online. Your bodily functions get super-sized, as new systems develop with infinite energy and infinite information available to the body.

> Everything that is happening is very centered in the physical body. It's beginning to open up into what we call a 'bio-transducer system.' Your body was designed to decode and work with Higher Light energies as well as transmit these energies to the planet.[50]

Description of the following levels of lightbody are based on the book, *What is Lightbody?* Many people are now at 3rd level lightbody, and from this point the stages become less linear. Remember, if you are having any of these symptoms, it is a natural part of lightbody evolution.

4th level lightbody goes from the physical to mental stages, firing up the electromagnetic factors in your brain. It includes non-linear thinking, choosing a personal reality paradigm, ego control battle, and accepting a vaster picture of reality- including multi-dimensionality. There is a "descension" of Spirit; the higher dimensional aspects of your Self come to live in your body to help you with the emotional transition of learning to be the vastness of Spirit. "I am here!" it says, and you become a joyful dance of Spirit showing up. 5th and 6th levels of lightbody get even more challenging and interesting.

In 7th level lightbody you have connected to the planet and "...you begin to experience NOW."[51] You enter the emotional stages of transformation. The heart chakra opens more and assists the merging of the emotional, mental and spiritual energy bodies. "If the heart chakra takes predominance... the chakra system merges into what we call the Unified Chakra. (Included in Practices) It's a unified energy field. It feels wonderful."[52] This grid includes your 14 chakras, important to unite so the forming lightbody can handle any amount of energy without damage to the physical form; the entire field holds the energy.

A gate to dimensions opens through the heart. The pineal and pituitary glands open, and the pineal develops a multi-dimensional 4th Eye.

Spiritual ambition may kick in, where the mental body is trying to find a form for following Spirit. One may adopt the identity as a healer or awakener, saving the planet, and then run themselves ragged trying to get others to follow their program.

You begin to function in a non-dual state of ecstasy as you hold both poles (your finite, together with the vast infinite part of your being) in the same container of "you." One is concerned about survival and the other focuses on the eternal One of the Spirit. You bounce back and forth trying to reconcile these two selves but can't; you hold both in the wide open container of "you" and stay in the middle of the paradox... in ecstasy.

You may experience yourself in other dimensions, or in other bodies on the planet. "You may have flashes of being in simultaneous time, where you are so NOW, you are all "NOW"s at once."[53] You are aware of probabilities and possibilities of everything you do; "...more aware of your connections with other people and of how deep your connection is with Spirit at any given moment."[54] Your feeling of: *I'm going to ascend tomorrow, I'm outa here...* is your current connection to your future self, that part of you that is already a lightbody.

At the end of this stage, you realize you are here for the long haul, by choice, to help others on the planet. There is a deep sense of purpose and service, of love for God and all life, and gratitude for your role.

<u>8th level lightbody</u> is one of the most transformative levels, with increased multi-dimensionality, but parallel realities as well. New pathways are created and you are aware of your vastness. New languages of light are going into your DNA. You are hooking up to multi-dimensional Mind...the point of going HOME. You experience geometrics, tones, and language of light or light codes are downloaded, which will make sense in a verbal manner at the next stage. Once again, you may not experience this or not be aware you are experiencing it at very deep or subtle levels.

Spirit directs you; you need no reasons or rationales, but follow Spirit with every breath and footstep. You interact with others because Spirit guides you to; words are from your Spirit. Peace and consistent ecstasy exist as you remain connected to your Spirit, and don't drift in and out.

You may feel you are going crazy; your nervous system is tweaked up to handle new levels of information and energy. A fifth-dimension axial system is coming online and merging with your autonomic nervous system; your heart begins to operate from the axial system. Light-workers develop a Group Mind at the 8th level of lightbody, a super highway to Source for new programs in service to the planet.

<u>In levels 9-12 lightbody,</u> a final letting go of the "I" happens. "You are beginning to embody Divinity."[55] First, you embody the Christ-consciousness, then the "I AM" Godself, and finally... the Cosmic-Self.

...you begin the final surrender to Spirit. Spirit designs everything: you are a divine instrument. It is a dissolution of the ego-self. This is the final passage through the gate of awakening. I am never separated from Source: I *am* Source. That is what is offered to each and every one of you, but it does mean surrender at every level of your being. Ninth level is where that surrender occurs, surrender and ecstasy."[56] At these highest levels of lightbody one experiences Avatar abilities, creates a merkabah, and comes and goes as a sometimes visible Master of the universe!

Final Stages: Outer Enlightenment

According to *The Human Body of Light* author, a board-certified psychiatrist investigating lightbody, four events mark the *outer* body's transformation into lightbody during the final phase of enlightenment. Most aspirants will hide themselves away from the public during these phases.

"*Gnosis/Logia*: The soul begins to tap into the knowledge contained within the Actus. Essentially, one becomes able to tap into the knowledge of the universe without prior study. The Actus region of the soul contains all the information of the universe. It also encodes the events which have and will transpire within the life of the soul. As the Gnostic process advances, one becomes able to literally know everything.

Aura: The soul begins to tap into the life force of the Creator himself. The soul gradually begins to emit visible light. The light however does not merely illuminate the body, it serves several functions. The light is capable of healing at a very high level: at its highest level, this light can restore life to a dead or dying form. The aura allows for the transformation of the body into a perfected form. The aura also causes certain miraculous phenomena such as bilocation, transubstantiation of matter, and the creation of living things. The aura is a sign that the Divine Ego is in the process of completely taking over the soul functions within a physical body. At the end of this process, the body glows with a supernal light after the point of death.

Levitia: During this phase of the enlightenment process, the Divine Ego guides the soul in the development of mastery over the laws of time and space. Essentially, the soul begins to lose its illusory connections with matter. As a result, the body begins to float, sometimes spontaneously. The flow of time and space is altered around the body and the aspirant often appears to be in another world, slightly out of phase with our own. A host of other phenomena accompany this stage of development.

Inedia: During this phase of development, the soul begins to nourish the body directly, without the need for food or water. The body subsists on the energy it draws indirectly from the universe. The process of inedia allows the body to live for longer and longer periods of time without conceding to its base needs, and signals the final phase of enlightenment in which the body begins to become self-generating. The body gradually loses its dependence on matter for its existence and begins to generate its own cells and structure from the fabric of the Creator. After the completion of this process, the body need no longer be born through the use of biological parents. The body is then fully enlightened and may generate itself at any time and at any place it desires. It is then ready for life in the higher realms of existence."[57]

Chapter 9: Practices for Evolving into Cosmic Beings

The final stage of mastery on this planet is learning practices to achieve mastery of Light, cultivation and expression of Light. Whether this development takes only one more single lifetime or thousands more lifetimes may simply be a matter of your belief, and your dedication to the process. Only advanced spiritual beings have ascended in the past. However, at a designated percentage of enlightenment on this planet, it could be the Divine Plan for humanity as a whole to accomplish this final return to Light- connection to the greater matrix.

As we evolve into cosmic beings, entering the gateway to life eternal, we develop an intense relationship with Light. We cultivate and harness our energy bodies by invoking, communing with, and projecting Light. The lightbody births at your highest potential, your highest Self, and leads to your infinite potential as a cosmic being.

The lightbody is for the next stages of our journey, where we resonate in harmony with the universe. This vehicle has been depicted as the Merkabah in Egyptian and Jewish mysticism, and the Microcosmic Orbit pearl in Taoist mysticism. It is an energetic container or vehicle for consciousness projection. By infusing both consciousness and Light together within the body in sacred alchemy, merging their energy information, we bring consciousness into our spirit or lightbody core. Since light moves through space easily, consciousness can travel in light and project outside the body into the universe. We can journey through various layers of existence, exploring the universe.

In the past, these highly esoteric practices for revving up our systems were taught in secret mystery schools. Fortunately, today they are available to independent students.

Taoists honor "Chi" as the supreme quintessential element. Chi is life-force, nature, flow and rhythm, the connecting and harmonizing field in the universe. Spiritual Chi-Gong practices instill awareness of this energy in our body: cultivating, tonifying, circulating, clearing, transforming, and storing it. The highest practice is cultivating the "pearl" or lightbody using the Microcosmic Orbit.

Within Taoist thought, rivers of energy called meridian pathways flow in the body, and wire the body to a Higher Force (Tao). This ancient knowledge is essentially what scientists in the bio-photonic research labs are investigating. To cultivate lightbody or The Golden Body, you connect with the waters of life and its different aspects of flow... interior flow, the flow of nature, and the flow of universal harmony. The more you stay in the flow, the more life-force (Light) you contain, and your life becomes incredibly effortless.

The Microcosmic Orbit is a highly esoteric Taoist practice, infusing levels of consciousness into a pearl, an energy body of condensed white light. You increase your frequency by circulating the energy faster thru the microcosmic orbit in your body. This is a continuous channel that goes up your back as yang and down your front as yin, and spins your chakras all at once. Once all chakras are accelerated, you can psychically thrust the pearl you have created in a specified manner up through your chakras and out your crown.

This also balances the masculine and feminine energies in your system. Cells have an electrical charge. Yin is a magnetic force bringing things together, like gravity. Yang is a bio-electrical force, like kinesthetic movement.

There must be a balance of yin and yang within the body to fire up the lightbody, an equalizing of inward and outward currents, and the merging of co-creative opposites. "The great secret of alchemy is the Divine Marriage of opposites which gives birth to the Spirit Body of transcendence associated with liberation of the soul."[58]

Before beginning practice of the Microcosmic Orbit, to be effective with this technique you must first master simple exercises to enhance your lightbody and hone control of energy.

A synchronistic event happened just as I began writing my thesis on lightbody. As I discovered the pearl phenomena in the Microcosmic Orbit, and found it amazingly interesting, a friend insisted I attend the Buddhist Relics. I agreed to go, despite having no clue what "relics" were; I thought relics were antique religious items! I learned Buddhist relics, found in cremation ashes of highly evolved and compassionate teachers, were the same "pearls" mentioned in the Orbit- the remnants of lightbodies. This exhibit ended up being visible and tangible proof for me that matter and consciousness can be fused. Intense consciousness filled the entire room, projecting peace and love from the former masters of the pearls.

When I arrived, the atmosphere of holiness and peace beyond understanding immediately settled over me. My David Hawkins Group friends reported: "This is resonating at level 700!" (Based on Hawkins' chart of consciousness) Indeed, one could hardly stand up in the room with all the grace present. Everyone else in the crowded room apparently felt it as well; many were sitting down meditating, walking slowly in a circle around the altar, or standing in awe by one of the relics on the tables.

The pearls were infused with the highest levels of consciousness from lifetimes of incredible mastery, compassion and service. Included in the tour were pearls of Gautama Buddha, donated by the Dalai Lama himself. When I walked up to the display with Gautama Buddha's pearls, I almost crumpled to my knees. It was the feeling of divine Presence, of receiving a great blessing.

The Merkabah is mentioned in many ancient cultures including Vedic, Egyptian and Jewish, as a lightbody vehicle. It is even conjectured to be used for UFO inter-dimensional travel. With scientists currently supporting theories of multi-dimensionality, and with our current body density unable to exist in them, it makes sense to develop a lightbody as the next step of evolution to house our galactic beings.

The universal vehicle, called the "Merkabah" ("Mer"= Light, The Energy that Connects the Two. "Ka" = Spirit, Angelic, and "Ba" = Earthly, Physical Body) is a self-created light-driven travel vehicle actually dating back to Indian Vedic texts. These vehicles of light or inter-dimensional vehicles were described as Vimanas or flying machines, and Hindu Gods and Goddesses are often depicted as flying in these chariots.

Considered a field of light energy around the physical body, "A Merkabah contains the sacred geometry that transcends all dimensions, time, and space. It has spiraling energy and counter-rotating spinning fields of light that can transport the body to another dimension and frequency."59 By imagining two superimposed star tetrahedrons, and with the help of certain mudras and breathing techniques, these can be activated into an invisible saucer shaped energy field around the human body.

Within the body, a concentration of light energy increases vibratory rate, resulting in a pulsating higher frequency. These individuals may begin to vibrate at a frequency higher than that of the third-dimension, shifting into dimensions of less density, the fifth-dimension or higher realms of light planes.

In practicing both the Merkabah and the Microcosmic Orbit, your internal universe expands to contain more Chi or life-force as you become aware of the entire universe resting within you. You create a vehicle which will connect you to the universe and all other beings, an energetic container to hold awareness and consciousness. As you shift in consciousness to experience your Self as energy and Light, there is an expanded awareness of Presence within. Then, you simply step into your lightbody and begin living a more universal existence. Ascended Masters are said to travel the universe in Merkabahs.

There is also the notion of a Merkabah around the earth, as part of her noospere and protective shield. The energy sheath or Web of Light that incases earth is known as the Crystalline Grid, or Matrix. As this Web of Light activates fully, so the Merkabahs will activate around the physical bodies on the earth.

Communing with Light

"O Light within, lighting my path to peace,

I adore and love You and I let You shine.

Go forth and bless all who come to You,

Light within.

My Light radiates to all and through all.

My light has come."

~ *Ernest Holmes, founder of Science of Mind*

To have direct experience of the Greater Reality, of Source, we experience and react with it as Light in our daily lives. "Communing" with Light is an intentional practice where the more you focus on Light, you are living in the Light, and you become Light. As we start living in Light, which is the Presence of God, it begins to radiate and work through us. Communing with Light is experiencing it in meditation as complete awareness of the Presence of God, with the intention of carrying that awareness forward into daily life. Communion is actually effortless if we relax, AND GET OUT OF THE WAY, since our essence wants to return to the Light, our true Selves.

The next step in evolution is to experience the awareness of Light as a divine gift available at this time. Use Light in daily life to tune into Higher Intelligence, power, and wisdom for self and others. Talk to light as you would with any other person. Light responds; and you will know it as you begin to pay attention.

...As the physical body holds and radiates
more Light, it fires up inner transmutation, and
we become light-bodies at the physical
level. Higher faculties are activated, dimensions
opened, and when many individuals radiate light
and its qualities... the Light Age manifests on
earth.[61]

Bringing more Light into your consciousness can be as easy as inviting and visualizing it. "Therefore I tell you, whatever you ask for in prayer, believe that you have received it, and it will be yours." (Mark 11:24) When we ask for Light and love the Light, it guides us by intuition... on *any* problem. As light increases and darkness vanishes, we start living in light, and manifest divine qualities like love, peace, and oneness.

One famous invocation for Light is Muhammad's Prayer on Light. There are several versions:

O Allâh, place light in my heart, light in my
tongue, light in my hearing, light in my sight,
light behind me, light in front of me, light on my

right, light on my left, light above me and light
below me; place light in my sinew, in my flesh, in
my blood, in my hair and in my skin; place light
in my soul and make light abundant for me;
make me light and grant me light.[62]

If readers wish to begin invoking Light, to pump up
the cells with Light and help the lightbody release, consider also invoking a violet light. (See Practices) Some
feel it can dissolve and consume, transmute and release
all negativity in our mental, emotional and etheric bodies. Violet has the highest vibration or frequency of all
visible colors, and our goal is to raise our frequency, and
also to clean up our other bodies.

Invoking Light produces an intense mystical state,
taking us from the intellectual to deep heart feelings.
Develop your own way of communing with Light. There
are many invocations for Light in various traditions. A
simple prayer works wonders: "I invoke the Light of God
within. I am a clear and perfect channel. Light is my
Guide."[63] This prayer was tested by a douser, and repeat-
ing it caused the energy field of the person to double.

There are invocations to form a tube or pillar of light
around you, sealing out discordant energies, there are
meditations where you picture your heart's golden-light
filling up your chest and overflowing into the shimmer-
ing light outside your body, forming a union.

Light Channeling The first time I tried channeling
Light was by connecting with the Light Channels in India. My temperature rose, and I was frozen to the spot
for hours, filled with Light. I didn't know how to release
it! In communing or invoking Light it's like a gentle
stream, but in channeling Light it is like a river flowing
through you to cover the earth!

Guruji Krishnananda and Light Channeling Volun-
teers have taught hundreds of thousands of children in
Indian schools, more than 27 lakhs in 4,900 schools, to

channel Light. Of these, roughly half a million children at 1,200 schools continue it channel Light daily as part of morning meditation.[64] (1 lakh= 100 thousand)

The simple technique that can even be instructed to children, is to picture an ocean of light above you, let it flow as if entering a funnel into your crown chakra, then expand it in your chest and fill your entire body; finally, release it and radiate Light to your surroundings and the planet.

When I did this, fully believing I was downloading God's Divine Light, I became transfixed to the spot. At the end of the day, I finally called a Hindu professor I knew, and she informed me of another woman who had to go to the emergency room because her temperature went up so high. Like me, she did not release the Light fast enough. I wrote her "remedy" on 3X5 cards, which I carried in my purse a long time, but it has never happened again.

I began to channel Light in rooms, in groups, and to the planet. I was an American liaison with Guruji before he passed, promoting his events nationally on the internet, and organized an event in Sedona.

No matter your age, light channels are those human beings who voluntarily channel and spread the Light, bringing the Light from its subtler level to the human level. Light channeling is spreading love, peace and harmony inherently carried by numinous light, dispersing its healing energies. It is recommended to channel light for 7 minutes in the morning and in the night.

Hidden Factors of Sunlight

Interacting with "X-factor" is a curious anomaly. The hidden factors in prana have been investigated, and may be useful for lightbody development. Why has it been a long-standing tradition for yogis to meditate at sunrise and sunset? Primary life- force energy is concentrated in the atmosphere at these times; it is called "X-factor." Released for about one hour after sunrise and during the hour before sunset, it is an extremely powerful force that may be stored within the brain, and causes a great change within the body. Lightbody is said to be activated by X-factor absorption.

As the energy of X-Factor increases within the body, the energy flow within the chakras increases and the dormant energy of the Life Force Centers is released. As the human mind evolves and enlightens, the planes of awareness expand and the Higher Mind gradually takes up residence within the physical body. The action of the X-factor makes this transition possible. As the (junk) DNA is transformed and decoded, the body and mind are transformed as well.[65]

Similar mystical and spiritual factors of prana have been explored since ancient times. There exist hidden aspects to the light of the sun linked to man's higher evolution. "Cultures as diverse as the Essenes, the Mayan, Aztecs, Buddhists, Hindus, Oceanic Tribes, and Native Americans all link the power of the sun to man's higher nature and evolution."[66]

Gibson's research on the hidden factors of sun reveal five major components of sunlight: Information Factors, Universal Forces, Evolutionary Factors, Energetic Factors, and Enlightenment Factors. The Ancients believed that these energies affect humans in a variety of ways; their knowledge of these energies was extensive. There are at least five main universal forces that are transmitted via the Sun throughout the Solar system. These forces are A-factor, B-Factor, X-factor, Y-factor, and Z-factor. Each of these factors play a specific role in our daily dimensional existence.

Sun-gazing for prana absorption is an ancient practice, and encouraged by some popular groups today

who stare directly into the sun during the first 20
minutes and last 20 minutes of the day. I hope more research is done on the safety and conversion of prana in
this technique.

Aspects of sunlight carry nourishing energy frequencies that are capable of sustaining life. All of the
elements that are necessary for life emanated originally
from the sun: water, air, fire, and earth, and all of the
necessary nutrients for life came to us from the sun. The
energetic factors that the sun releases are able to *become*
our bodies, without any other food, and only minimal
water intake. This is considered digestion of prana.
There are several thousand "prana-eaters" called
breatharians on the planet, and Indian Masters believe
highly advanced spiritual people will be able to switch
automatically to prana if it were necessary in the future.

Ascension

Ascension is a concept of much speculation in today's New Age community, although the idea has been
around forever. I feel the Light in our souls has quick-
ened our hearts, and because we love more our
lightbodies are activating.

Light is seen as living, intelligent, self-directed, co-
operative consciousness within the cells of our bodies
and extending into inner dimensions as well as the cosmos. It is the sticky-glue holding everything together, the
field in the Unified Field Theory. Light is seen as God, as
All-That-Is. It makes sense that Light is at our core, beneath the fleshy body, deep within hearts where only
unconditional love can reach and break it free. Unconditional love, meditation and Grace seem to play a major
role in the rate of transformation into lightbody and ascension as our true Selves.

Ascension literally means an act of rising to a higher
position, claiming our galactic solar bodies, and begin-

ning our role in the universe. Popular culture, perhaps through science-fiction and fantasy genres, will be lead to a realization that stepping into the next dimensional reality is a *natural* step, not a rare and bizarre event.

Energies are flooding the earth as our solar system and galaxy barrel along through new frontiers of space. Energies from the Photon Belt and Galactic Centre are entering our atmosphere. Both earthly and cosmic evolution are said to be accelerating due to our approaching a new place in the universe. Discovering new facts as they surface from fields such as astronomy, cosmology, and quantum physics, will explain how cosmic energy effects evolution as well as lightbody development.

I believe the lightbody is accelerating from cosmic forces, and from Grace. We are concluding the end of a 5,000 year period of darkness and the beginning of a Golden Age, or Light Age. One theory is we will be entering a field of strong spiritual energy, able to help us manifest love, compassion and oneness. Weaker and grosser energy fields will get annihilated, for they cannot co-exist. Those who hold such energy in their bodies will suffer and collapse, from conflict, confusion, and transmuting of lower energy.

Could the earth be ascending, too? We are interconnected and energetically tied to the earth, and many hold the theory that we are ascending together. They claim that as earth prepares to ascend, we need to prepare along with her. Every living thing that holds a similar vibration and is aligned will ascend alongside her when the time arrives. The theory is that the energies of third-dimensional earth will transmute into fifth-dimension, and as we shift into this new energy, we will have ascended. The third-dimension frequency on earth will no longer exist.

I feel that as the cosmic cycles and humanity's evolutionary course progress, it will get even easier with fewer qualifications to ascend. Once an individual has mastered their thoughts and emotions and is living in unconditional love, they will rise in frequency and simply disappear from physicality. It will just be like stepping through a portal into the Light. This ascension is the state of oneness with the Light. Yet it is important to see ascension as the completion stage of our existence. We should aspire towards it in our lives, but from day to day, moment to moment, we should focus upon our area of service.

As much as we want to reach enlightenment and ascend into higher planes of existence when our work is done here, the God power in the universe – we can call it the propensity toward perfection – holds even greater aspirations. So we have the Spirit of Guidance. And, we can invoke certain Masters to bestow their attributes we need in a particular situation.

Ascension isn't a unique opportunity not to die, but the path to enter immortal life as the endgame of linear time. Jesus' goal was to lead humanity to ascension. And returning to lightbody... is just the beginning!

SPIRIT OF LOVE by Bassouls

Much support exists for the possibility that the human body acts as a cocoon for a higher, more exotic form with the potential for immortality. There is certainly enough mythology about beings of Light, Masters who have ascended and inhabit invisible realms from which humanity can call to them for assistance. Every religion has such beings. But to say that *you and I* will progress to that state of ultimate mastery... is a hopeful, yet *possible* diagnosis for the human condition.

It is saying, "I believe every person is a Christ, a Buddha, capable of perfection and achieving full union with God." How different our social interactions would be if we all looked at each other as masters in the making! We would honor each other, and cease judging each other, knowing our souls have chosen enhancing experiences and roles of all sorts for us in this cosmic school called Earth.

The pre-requisites for transformation into lightbody seem steep. For most, it entails endless lifetimes of ardent self-reflection and gaining dominion over the physical, emotional, mental, and etheric bodies we wear over our soul like a spacesuit. But if there is no plan that such ardent endeavors to live up to our highest potential lead to a new paradigm, a more heavenly existence, what would be the point of creation? If not to learn, to accomplish, and to evolve?

According to a story about Jesus in the Essene community, some friends felt the masses of humanity should not be concerned with the lofty idea of ascension. "But a few, like John and James, and Thomas and Mary, and Mary Magdalene, were at one with Jesus on this. They said that if you do not put the Completion Stage before people they will not be able to aspire to it, and may spend many lives at lesser levels."[67] I agree, and my purpose in this book is to put this probability of returning to Light before the masses, and let those with ears hear, and have a clear-cut goal in mind.

If the process of lightbody development is more widely acknowledged in society, and techniques to unleash its potentiality are available, it would unite spiritual practitioners in a common, practical vision. If they could resonate with focusing on unleashing our bodies of Light, it would happen with exponential speed.

A very good question is often asked. "If in the beginning we were already this pure essence, this natural awareness, this Light, why has God gone to all this trouble?" Perhaps, it was intended for the One Power and Only Presence to experience life fully, including the unbounded joy and limitless knowing that occurs at the end... of merging back into Light. Or perhaps, lost in creation, God (We) have just forgotten WHO is here, always in the moment of the eternal now.

Besides the mystical and metaphysical questions of returning back into the Light of God, there is the physical proof that something indeed has transpired, as advanced human beings disperse their forms into rainbows of energy. All highly spiritual people today feel a profound shift occurring within their bodies. Meditators in deep states of *samadhi*, brought about by purity of mind and resting in their true nature, report intensely vibrating electro-magnetic energy. They experience increased flow of chi or Light. Our attention and intention can be applied methodically to creating internal alchemy for transmutation.

Perhaps society can understand manifesting lightbody better as a science. They could examine the process as octaves of frequency, ascending and descending stages and states, dimensions, and levels of consciousness.

Or possibly, we can explain this process to society as an adventure story in the gaming industry; they will buy it, and seek the changes in character that promote spirituality. "The Awakening of the Body of Light" is the theme. We are each the hero on a quest for the treasure...the Resurrection Body hidden inside the physical body.

Yahya Sohravardi, the great mystic and reviver of Hermetic gnosis in Islam, had at the heart of his ideology the recognition that the" I" of every self-aware entity is a pure, immaterial light. He believed we have a partner, our own Higher Self, a "Man of Light" within. He comes with a built-in Spirit of Guidance, the heavenly "I," an eternal partner and companion.[68]

This idea is taken from the Greeks: Prometheus is the man of light, held captive by darkness and struggling to free himself from darkness, but oriented toward light as he follows his own Guide of light. The manifestation of perfect nature must occur in his living experience of the cosmic adventure, the unity of the Man of Light and his Guide. The couple comes to be joined in the end.

This Spirit of Guidance assists us in following the path to our Perfect Nature, divine blueprint or Adam Kadmon. When the game is over, this process liberates the Man of Light. The perfect ending!

Most beloved One:
Our hearts are like magnets.
We meet in that place
Where I am losing myself in you,
And you are losing yourself in me,
And only one of us is doing this dance,
And it doesn't matter who.
Joy has no name,
And no boundaries...

From the book *Return to Oneness*
By Cynthia Clayton

JOURNEY HOME by Rassouli

Closing

Thank you Spirit of Guidance! Writing this book has been a journey of embodiment of my soul, experiencing Light within my own being in a whole new way. I am grateful for receiving knowledge I never would have found without the Spirit of Guidance. It took us to the core of the magical human being, to the Heart of the Light within all spiritual traditions.

I hope this book has led you on a journey. Who doesn't love a mystery uncovered, and the promise of eternal life? If you already had the realization that we are in the days of birthing our highest eternal Selves, you may now have the added clarity that this is a uniting of Soul and Spirit. It is a transfiguration, resurrection and ascension out of flesh into Divine nature. We are not held back any longer by the cycle of birth and death, as all karma can be reconciled, purified and released. The soul's journey is reaching completion. The Genie emerges from the lamp, with no need to return!

The lightbody process has thought-provoking factors to explore, many of which I've touched upon. New findings in research on bio-photons in the human body support the acupuncture energy grid used since ancient times, supporting a Body of Light. We have examined how energy flows as a frequency in the nervous system, transmuting us and causing unexplainable symptoms in the process. I have suggested that we are cosmic beings, and can propel our consciousness attached to Light, directing it in a lightbody vehicle.

We have located Home, our highest frequency, the state obtained by the Buddhist Dzogchen and other meditators. It is absolute reality- yet emptiness; the transparency of primordial non-dual awareness. It is spotlessly pure and indestructible, the clear-light of un-differentiated consciousness, the highest samadhi to which we can aspire before passing through the Door.

Lightbody is the explanation of immortality. That every tradition in the world has the archetype of a lightbody, but has kept it hidden in mystery schools, is because the timing was not right for its realization. Humans have been living a very backward existence! It would have been casting pearls before swine. The right time is Now, because finally, we understand where Now is.

My goal in this writing has been to try and recover for humanity some very profound truths about who we are as human beings. To broaden our scope of what we believe is possible. To help readers manifest their highest potential. And, to realize the driving force of evolution is a sacred alchemy deep inside of us, birthing gold from lead by uniting conscience and consciousness.

I feel there are many old souls, bodhisattvas, who have returned many times to be Light-workers, raise consciousness, and dispel negative energies, and it is their time to take everyone Home on their coattails. They are holding open the Door. And while in the past everyone seemed to be swimming upstream, the cosmic energies of Grace are allowing all Light to flow gently back into the Light now. I feel the Light of Creation has won!

Jesus told us that there comes a point in the
development of every human being when
the soul is filled with a great longing for the
Light. At that point, everything the world can
offer seems hollow and worthless. The only
thing that will then satisfy the soul is to return to
the Light from whence it came, and merge with
that Light and become one with it.[69]

AND SO IT IS!

Practices

Find your own! Make some up! These are just a sample.

Invocation to Light

I live within the Light.
I love within the Light.
I laugh within the Light.

I AM sustained and nourished
by the Light.
I joyously serve the Light.
For
   I AM the Light
   I AM the Light.
   I AM the Light.

I AM. I AM. I AM.

***   ***   ***

Raise Your Vibration

There are many ways to raise our vibration. The most important thing we can do right now is state our intention.

I am ready to raise my vibration, integrating the energies of the Christ Consciousness into my being with ease and grace and for my highest good.

Stating your intention every day, shifting your thoughts and beliefs, getting in touch with your feelings, releasing toxic emotions, integrating the ego, overcoming shadow consciousness, as well as daily meditation are the most important things you can do.

TIPS

1) Do something meaningful for a total stranger without putting judgments on whether or not they deserve it, and of course, without expectation of reward. And do it anonymously! You will be amazed at how great this feels. (Pay someone's restaurant tab, take someone's newspaper up to their porch, put some money in an envelope and put it on someone's windshield with a note "You are loved," pick some flowers from your garden and take them to a nursing home to be given to someone of the administration's choosing. The ideas are endless!) When you are a conduit for divine blessings, you are automatically raised in frequency.

2) GO OUTSIDE! Go out in nature and instead of expecting nature to rejuvenate and nurture you, consciously transmit your love and appreciation to nature. Zap! Up in frequency you go!

3) Say "thank you." Visit, call, or write someone to thank them for a kindness—even one from long ago. They'll be thrilled to hear it and you'll feel wonderful, too. Gratitude is powerful.

4) Breathe! Just by taking some deep, conscious breaths, you will find yourself in a clearer space. When you imagine yourself rising higher with each breath, you will!

5) When you find yourself under stress, put your hand over your heart "Pledge of Allegiance" style. It will calm and center you. A calm, centered person's frequency is always higher than a freaked out, scattered person's! Smile to your heart.

6) Step outside, take in some fresh air, and let the sun kiss your face (even on a cloudy day, the sun is still there, though invisible to our eyes). This one is SO simple, but how often have we forgotten to do it?!

7) Say a heartfelt "thank you" to your Spirit for anything that occurs in your life, even—no, *especially*—that

which you aren't too thrilled about! (You know that when something inharmonious occurs, it's a signpost that alerts you that you have wandered off course so that you can navigate yourself back to alignment!) Gratitude puts you back in alignment and raises your frequency.

8) Look at yourself in the mirror and smile!

9) Hug yourself and say "I love you" to YOU on behalf of your Spirit!

10) Last, but most importantly of all, consciously, unconditionally radiate Love to all Creation. This is your primary job as a human being, and you are hard-wired to do it, so no instruction should be necessary, but here's a hint: it will be easier to do if you center yourself in your heart and do the breathing exercise in #4 first!

*** *** ***

11 QUICK AND SIMPLE WAYS TO RAISE YOUR VIBRATION

1. Take a bath or shower, or if time is of the essence, submerge your hands in a sink of water or run water over your hands for several minutes. Water itself is of a higher vibration and it has an amazing ability to lift our vibration. Simply being in the vicinity of a body of water will raise our vibration. Immersing our body or hands within water is an easy and effective means of raising your vibration. I always find that washing dishes has an uncanny way of lifting my spirits!

2. Focus upon your breathing, inhaling deeply and exhaling fully. No matter where you are or what you may be doing, this is a simple, yet very effective way to raise your vibration. By bringing more oxygen into your body, you are energizing each cell within it and in particular infusing your brain with life giving oxygen. Physically you

will feel more energized and within minutes you will feel your overall vibration shift to a higher level.

3. Recall and relive a wonderful experience from your past. Choose a memory that filled you with joy at the time and take a few moments to mentally relive it. Your vibration responds the same whether you are simply imagining it. The 'feeling place' you reach is the only thing of importance.

4. Daydream about manifesting a future desire. Really get into the feeling place of experiencing the joy and satisfaction that the manifestation of a specific desire will bring. Revel in the knowing that the positive feeling the imagined manifestation of this desire brings, is the very vehicle through which it is making its way into your present moment experience. The better you feel, the more good stuff is coming!

5. If it's sunny outside, face the sun, close your eyes and allow the sun to bathe you. Focus upon the inside of your eyelids and the colors you see there. Bask in the warmth and feeling of soul nourishment the sun provides.

6. Remove your socks and shoes and walk on grass. This is a great means of 'grounding' your physical energy and raising your overall vibration. Take a few moments to focus upon the sensation of your own energy merging with the energy of the ground you stand upon. This exercise works wonderfully to raise your vibration when combined with basking in the sun.

7. Take a glass of water, bless it and infuse it with your highest, most positive intentions and then drink it. Water has an amazing ability to absorb our vibrations and intents. It reacts to our intentions like a chameleon reacts to colors. It takes on whatever properties we infuse it with.

8. Wear clothing made of natural fibers that feel good against your skin. Put on a favorite piece of jewelry

or clothing. When we surround ourselves with things we like we are raising our vibration.

9. Smile. Regardless of how you are currently feeling, purposefully form your mouth into the most realistic smile you possibly can. If need be, imagine something funny or something that makes smiling easy. (I find the memory of my dog or children engaging in something silly or cute works well). Don't force the emotions, but allow them to evolve along with a smile that is genuine. Allow the smile to move throughout your body. Feel your heart 'smile.' Feel your solar plexus 'smile.' Right now, believe it or not, my toes are smiling....feels great!

10. Caress your pet or hug a child. Most children and animals naturally exude a high vibration. When we physically engage with them in a conscious manner, some of their energy naturally rubs off on us. This may sounds a bit like vampire-ism, however, most of us experience a surge in loving energy when we engage with those we feel love and affection towards. When this happens, we create a continuous circuit of high vibration and our child or pet will also benefit from the energy exchange!

11. Listen to music that makes your heart soar. If possible...Dance! It's impossible to dance to your favorite music and not shift your vibration to a higher level.

Basically, any activity that causes us to feel enjoyment will have the power to shift our vibration and bring us to a vibrational reality where we can more easily manifest our desire. The real pay-off though will be in our present moment experience of greater levels of joy!

*** *** ***

MORE!

1) Smile. The moment we smile we release negative energy. Even if we don't feel like smiling, the physical act of doing so relaxes our muscles and makes it impossible to cling to all the yuckiness trapped in our scowl. Smiling flips an invisible switch, creating just enough movement and space inside with which to un-stick ourselves. There is a reason Buddha is always smiling.

2) Pray. By "pray" I don't mean say our hail Mary's (whatever that even means), I mean closing our eyes and focusing on a wish of peace for ourselves and all the creatures of the world—particularly those creatures which might have been annoying you lately; teenaged offspring, corrupt world leaders, the cashier at the grocery store.)

3) Have a mantra. I consider mantras emergency kits for when I'm too frazzled to think things through and I need to set the ship straight. "May we be free from suffering and the cause of suffering." "May all beings be safe, may all beings be well, may all beings be happy, may all beings be free. May I be safe, may I be well, may I be happy, may I be free." "The light of God surrounds me, the power of God protects me, the love of God enfolds me, the presence of God watches over me. Where ever I am, God is."

4) Breathe. We hear this instruction so often it's almost become a cliché. Nevertheless, focusing on the physical reality of the breath is always a great away to go. By focusing on the breath, we are turning off the mind and all of its unproductive chattering and tuning back into the *self*, which is a place of peace and wisdom.

Don't let the ego tell you that "just breathing" isn't going to accomplish anything. Our breath is the thread which moors us to the present moment. Experiencing this moment in its beautiful, visceral simplicity is the ultimate way to raise our vibration. Try the Birthing Breath!

5) 7 sets of rubbing palms together. 7 times each set.

6) Mudra "I GIVE UP." "I" (hands on heart), "GIVE" (hands down toward ground), "UP!" (hands up over head, eyes follow hands)

7)Toning. Be a siren- start as low as possible to as high as possible, say "WHOOOOOOOO"

*** *** ***

Ascended Master Saint Germain's Meditation

Feel your body enveloped in a dazzling white light. Feel your heart become a golden ball of light. Let it flare up into a radiant ball of light like a sun. Picture it getting bigger and bigger and filling your entire chest, filling your entire body. Feel it merge with the dazzling white light around you, the field of light that is All-That-Is, that is the Love of the Universe surrounding you. We are all connected in this field of energy.

Now, we are going to super-size our feeling. Repeat three times: "I joyfully accept the fullness of the mighty Christ." Feel every cell in your body tingling with the light that exists there. Send thanks and blessings to every photon. Ending:

"I AM a child of the light.

I love the light.

I serve the light.

I live in the Light.

I am protected, illumined, supplied and sustained by the light.

And I bless the light!"

*** *** ***

Invocation to the Unified Chakra

"I breathe in Light
Through the center of my heart,
Opening my heart
Into a beautiful ball of Light,
Allowing myself to expand.

I breathe in Light
Through the center of my heart,
Allowing the Light to expand,
Encompassing my throat chakra
And my solar plexus chakra
In one unified field of Light
Within, through, and around my body.

I breathe in Light
Through the center of my heart,
Allowing the Light to expand,
Encompassing my brow chakra
And my navel chakra
In one unified field of Light
Within, through, and around my body.

I breathe in Light
Through the center of my heart,
Allowing the Light to expand,
Encompassing my crown chakra
And my base chakra
In one unified field of Light
Within, through, and around my body.

I breathe in Light
Through the center of my heart,
Allowing the Light to expand,
Encompassing my Alpha chakra

(Eight inches above my head)
And my Omega chakra
(Eight inches below my spine)
In one unified field of Light
Within, through, and around my body.
I allow a Wave of Highest Consciousness
To move between two these points.
I AM a unity of Light.

I breathe in Light
Through the center of my heart,
Allowing the Light to expand,
Encompassing my eighth chakra
(Above my head)
And my upper thighs
In one unified field of Light
Within, through, and around my body.
I allow my emotional body to merge
With my physical body.
I AM a unity of Light.

I breathe in Light
Through the center of my heart,
Allowing the Light to expand,
Encompassing my ninth chakra
(Above my head)
And my lower thighs
In one unified field of Light
Within, through, and around my body.
I allow my mental body to merge
With my physical body.
I AM a unity of Light.

I breathe in Light
Through the center of my heart,
Allowing the Light to expand,
Encompassing my tenth chakra

(Above my head)
And my knees
In one unified field of Light
Within, through, and around my body.
I allow my spiritual body to merge
With my physical body,
Forming the unified field.
I AM a unity of Light.

I breathe in Light
Through the center of my heart,
Allowing the Light to expand,
Encompassing my eleventh chakra
(Above my head)
And my upper calves
In one unified field of Light
Within, through, and around my body.
I allow the Oversoul to merge
With the unified field.
I AM a unity of Light.

I breathe in Light
Allowing the Light to expand,
Encompassing my twelfth chakra
(Above my head)
And my lower calves
In one unified field of Light
Within, through, and around my body.
I allow the Christ Oversoul to merge
With the unified field.
I AM a unity of Light.

I breathe in Light
Through the center of my heart,
Allowing the Light to expand,
Encompassing my thirteenth chakra
(Above my head)

And my feet
In one unified field of Light
Within, through, and around my body.
I allow the I AM Oversoul to merge
With the unified field.
I AM a unity of Light.

I breathe in Light
Through the center of my heart,
Allowing the Light to expand,
Encompassing my fourteenth chakra
(Above my head)
And to below my feet
In one unified field of Light
Within, through, and around my body.
I allow the Source's Presence to move
Throughout the unified field.
I AM a unity of Light.

I breathe in Light
Through the center of my heart.
I ask that the highest level of my Spirit
Radiate forth
From my heart,
Filling this unified field completely.
I radiate forth throughout this day.
I AM a unity of Spirit."

From *What is Lightbody?* By Archangel Ariel and
Tashira Tachi-ren

*** *** ***

80

Activate Your Diamond Light Body

1. Quiet yourself, center your attention in your body, be in the present moment 100 percent, and create calmness and receptivity. Recall your list of positive experiences.

2. Imagine that behind your back, your diamond light body appears. This body looks just like you but is made of pure transparent light and has no wounds or blockages. Your light body radiates wisdom, love, harmony, and the knowledge of abundance. Your light body steps forward and puts its hands on your shoulders.

3. In your imagination, feel the higher vibration of your light body; welcome it and attune to the frequency. As you do, your light body steps inside you, merging with you seamlessly and easily.

4. Your light body matches up with your physical body perfectly, each light body part finding its physical body part: the light heart merges with the physical heart, the light cells match the physical cells, the light brain joins the physical brain. Take some time to scan through the various parts of your body as this process occurs.

5. Allow yourself to let go into the light body as it takes over, saying, "You know how to run this brain, this heart, these lungs, how to use these hands, this voice. Please show me how. I trust you to renew me, reorganize me, and teach me." Fall into your own light and feel supported.

6. An odd thing happens; as you let your diamond light body take over to guide you, a saturation point is reached where you "flip" and realize you are the diamond light body. Your identity shifts. As you hear the voice of guidance from the light body, you realize it's your voice. You might say, "I am here now, and I know what's real."

7. Let the diamond light saturate not only every cell, but your emotions, feelings, and thoughts as well. Let it

work on your brain and body, dissolving shadows, filling in gaps, upgrading all your systems, erasing worry and doubt, opening new pathways, and reprogramming you with updated frequencies. Remain in the silence.

8. Now, "strike the tuning fork" of your diamond light body's vibration and let waves of your light and your original tone ripple through every tiny space in your body and out through your skin into the space around you. Let it expand as far into the universe as it wants. As your own diamond light expands, it joins with the diamond light it encounters in the presence everywhere. In the center of the light, you can hear or feel your soul's eternal indestructible tone or home frequency.

By Penney Peirce, (2009-01-25). *Frequency*, Simon & Schuster, Inc. Kindle Edition.

*** *** ***

From KARIMA'S Violet Flame Collection

I honor all the original sources, but do not recall them as I have gathered these over the years. These are for the world!

Mighty "I AM" Presence, higher mental bodies of all mankind, all great beings, powers, and legions of light! Beloved Mighty Saint Germain!

Blaze your Violet Consuming Flame, the Purifying Power of Divine Love in, through, and around us! Purify all the substance and energy in my mental, emotional, and physical bodies! Quiet the whirls of vibratory action in my emotional body! Dissolve all impurities in the flesh, and consume all wrong thought patterns in my mental body! Increase the vibratory action of my mind and body, so the Currents of Light and Energy from my "Presence" flow-through in Perfect Balance, bringing ease in my feelings – raising, transforming, purifying, and vivifying the Activity of the Ascended Masters' Divine Love from the Heart of God, the "Mighty I AM Presence."

Come into Perfect Manifestation on Earth, swift as a flash, Perfect as the Ascended Masters see It! And in, through, and around all under this Radiation- descend!

I DEMAND THIS MANIFEST, MANIFEST, MANIFEST!
I EXPECT THIS MANIFEST, MANIFEST, MANIFEST!
IN ALL OUR VICTORY, VICTORY, VICTORY
ATTAINED RIGHT NOW!
ALMIGHTY I AM!
ALMIGHTY I AM!
ALMIGHTY I AM!

*** *** ***

"I AM" the Mighty Violet Consuming Flame that now and forever consumes all past and present mistakes, their cause, effect, record, and memory, and all undesirable creation for which my outer is responsible!

Doubled each hour, ruling in all God's Supremacy and Obedience, in all we ever do or contact, until all are Ascended and Free, and Right Now! This instant and forever descend!

Descend, Descend, Descend!

*** *** ***

"MIGHTY I AM PRESENCE," GREAT HOST OF ASCENDED MASTERS, MIGHTY LEGIONS OF LIGHT, GREAT ANGELIC HOST, GREAT COSMIC BEINGS, AND GREAT COSMIC LIGHT! IN THE NAME, LOVE,

WISDOM, POWER, AUTHORITY AND VICTORY OF OUR OWN BELOVED MIGHTY I AM PRESENCE, HIGHER MENTAL BODIES OF ALL MANKIND, AND ALL WHO DIRECT THE SACRED FIRE TO THIS EARTH!

I DEMAND, I COMMAND, I INSIST, AND "I AM" THAT "I AM PRESENCE," WHICH COMPELS! (3) AND FOREVER MAINTAINS, by Instantaneous Precipitation or otherwise, all Activities of the Sacred Fire and the most Boundless Love in the Universe!

*** *** ***

"BELOVED MIGHTY I AM PRESENCE" AND BELOVED SAINT GERMAIN! ALL ACTIVITIES OF THE SACRED FIRE, AND THE MOST BOUNDLESS LOVE IN THE UNIVERSE!

Clothe us in your Cosmic Mantle of Violet Consuming Flame, Power, Protection, Freedom, and Blessings! COMPEL! (3) Your Violet Consuming Flame to surge through this city and every home, person, place, condition, and thing within it: and dissolve and consume that which holds mankind in distress!

MANIFEST! (repeat 3 times)
Right now! This instant and forever!
ALMIGHTY I AM!
ALMIGHTY I AM!
ALMIGHTY I AM!

*** *** ***

84

SIMPLE TO MEMORIZE:

Transmute, transmute by Violet Fire,
all causes and cores not of God's desire,
I AM a Being of Cause alone,
that Cause is LOVE...
the Sacred Tone.

*** *** ***

I AM a Being of the Violet Fire, I AM the Purity God
desires. The earth is a Being of the Violet Fire, The earth
is the Purity God desires.

*** *** ***

In the Name I AM THAT I AM and my Beloved Holy
Christ Self!

"I AM" forgiveness for all,
For the Violet Fire we call
Now to make all discord cease
And through mercy's flame release
All that was not meant to be
Ever raise all back to Thee.

Violet Flame blaze up through me,
Remove all patterns not of Thee
Let love, compassion through me flow,
Perfection's light now aglow.
One with the freedom of the Great I AM
One with the freedom of the Great I AM
One with the freedom of the Great I AM

***　***　***

I AM the Violet Flame
In action in me now
I AM the Violet Flame
In mighty cosmic power
I AM the Light of God
Shining every hour
I AM the Violet Flame
Blazing like a sun
I AM God's sacred power
Freeing everyone.

(repeat 7 times, increasing in speed)

This genie is you

I AM THE
RESURRECTION
AND THE LIFE!

ENDNOTES

1. (Patel, 1208)
2. (Nyoshul, 1208)
3. (peterrussell.com/SG/Ch5.php)
4. (Bischof, 2)
5. (Newton, "Query 30" of the _Opticks_)
6. (Wilson and Prentis, 258)
7. (Hebrew 11:5)
8. (Holland, Quote by Father Francis Tiso)
9. (Krishnananda, Lightchannels website)
10. (Curtis and Hurtak, 27)
11. (Schwartz)
12. (Schwartz)
13. (Gospel of Thomas)
14. (Holden)
15. (Holden)
16. (Somayaji, 24)
17. (Somayaji, 27)
18. (Curtis and Hurtak, 32)
19. (Curtis and Hurtak, 28, Quote by Nobel laureate Dr. Albert Szent-Györgi (1960))
20. (Curtis and Hurtak, 27)
21. (Curtis and Hurtak, 34)
22. (Curtis and Hurtak, 32)
23. (Curtis and Hurtak, 32)
24. (Bischof, 1)
25. (Bischof, 2)
26. (Pennisi)
27. (Eddy)
28. (Max Planck, famous quote)

29. (Curtis and Hurtak, 28)
30. (Curtis and Hurtak, 34)
31. (Curtis and Hurtak, 28)
32. (Gurdjieff, Atomism, Wikipedia)
33. (Peirce, 49)
34. (Peirce, 49)
35. (Masters Lessons Vol. 1, 24)
36. (Peirce, 240)
37. (Hawking, Brief History of Time)
38. (Sagan, YouTube, 4th Dimension)
39. (Nyoshul and Barron, 38)
40. (Holland, Quote by Father Francis Tiso)
41. (Holland, Quote by Brother David Steindl-Rast)
42. (Holland, Quote by Brother David Steindl-Rast)
43. (Powers, 392)
44. (Norbu, 71)
45. (Norbu and Shane, Location 910)
46. (Norbu and Shane, Location 1109)
47. (Norbu and Shane Location 1457)
48. (Reynolds, 165)
49. (Thondup, 82)
50. (Tachi-ren, 45)
51. (Tachi-ren, 55)
52. (Tachi-ren, 56)
53. (Tachi-ren, 60)
54. (Tachi-ren, 60)
55. (Tachi-ren, 65)
56. (Tachi-ren, 67)
57. (Gibson, Location 1115-1135)
58. (Love)
59. (Patel, Location 1284)
60. (Patel, Location 1249)

61. (Amara, 40)
62. (Rabbani)
63. (Walker)
64. (Lightchannels.com, News)
65. (Gibson, Location 793)
66. (Gibson, Location 793)
67. (Wilson and Prentis, 260)
68. (Corbin)
69. (Wilson and Prentis, 261)

GRACE OF ALPHA by Rassouli

RESOURCES

Amara, Vishwa. Communing with Light, Techniques of Light for Everday Living. Vishwaamara.com. 2011. Free e-Book.

Barrett, Tom. "Chop Wood, Carry Water." www. interluderetreat.com. 2000. Web. 19 Feb.   2013.

Bischof, Marco. "Biophotons- The Light in Our Cells." International-light- association.eu. 2005. Web. 04 Mar. 2013.

Corbin, Henry. The Man of Light in Iranian Sufism. SanFrancisco:_Omega   Publications. 1994. Print.

Curtis, Bruce, and J.J. Hurtak. "Consciousness and Quantum Information Processing: Uncovering   the Foundation for a Medicine of Light." The Journal   of Alternative and Complementary Medicine 10.1 N.Y.: Mary Ann Liebert.   2004. Print. 27-39

Eddy, Sean. "The C-value Paradox, Junk DNA and ENCODE." Current Biology. N.p., 06 Nov. 2012. Web. 01 Mar. 2013.

Gibson, Mitchell, MD. The Human Body of Light. 1st Edition. High Point,   N.C.:   Tybro. 2010. Kindle.

Gospel of Thomas, Lambdin Translation. The Nag Hammadi Library. Gnosis.org. 1990. Web. 19 Feb. 2013.

Holden, Lee. Your Body of Light: Energetic Practices for Better Health, Emotional Balance, and Higher Consciousness. Louisville, CO: Sounds True. 2009, audio cd.

Holland, Gail. "Christian Buddhist Explorations of the Rainbow Body." Livedeepnow.com. IONS Review No.59, 2002. Web. 04 July 2015.

Holy Bible. New International Version. Bible.cc. Online Parallel Bible. 1984. Web. 04 Mar. 2013.

Krishnananda, Guruji. "What is Light."

Lightchannels.com. Manasa Foundation, 2012. Web. 12 Dec. 2012. Free e-Book.

"Light Therapy." Cancer.org. American Cancer Society. n.d. Web. 02 Mar. 2013.

Love, Arion. "Alchemy: The Science of Enlightenment," Ascendingstarseedwordpress.com. 08 Aug. 2012. Web. 02 Mar. 2013.

Masters, Paul. Masters Degree Level Lessons Volumes 1and 2. University of Metaphysics. 1989. Print.

Norbu, Namkhai. Dzogchen: The Self-Perfected State. Ithica, New York: Snow Lion. 1996. Kindle.

Norbu, Namkhai, and John Shane. The Crystal And The Way Of Light: Sutra, Tantra And Dzogchen. Ithica, New York: Snow Lion. 2000. Kindle.

Nyoshul, Khenpo, and Richard Barron. A Marvelous Garland of Rare Gems: Biographies of Masters of Awareness in the Dzogchen Lineage; a Spiritual History of the Teachings of Natural Great Perfection. Junction City, CA: Padma. 2005. Print.

Patel, Jal. Expect A Miracle Of Ascension: Plus 24 Steps to a Miracle Conscious That Guarantee Spiritual and Human Excellence Bloomington, IN: Balboa, 2011. Kindle.

Peirce, Penney. Frequency: The Power of Personal Vibration. Hillsboro, OR: Beyond Words, 2011. Kindle.

Pennisi, Elizabeth. "ENCODE Project Writes Eulogy for Junk DNA." Science. 1159-161. 07 Sept. 2012. Web. 01 Mar. 2013.

Powers, John. Introduction to Tibetan Buddhism. Ithaca, NY: Snow Lion. 2007. Print.

Rabbani, Faraz. "The Dua of Light." Spa.qibla.com. Quibla, n.d. Web. 2 March 2013.

Rabjam, Longchen. The Practice of Dzogchen. Ithica, NY:Snow Lion. 2002. Print.

Reynolds, John. The Golden Letters. Ithica, NY: Snow Lion. 1996. Print.

Schwartz, Howard. "How the Ari Created a Myth and Transformed Judaism." Tikkun.org. 28 March 2011. Web. 05 July 2015.

Somayaji, Raghavendra. Light Body and Other Realities. Bangalore: Manasa Light Age Foundation. 2012. Print.

Tachi-ren, Tashira, and Archangel Ariel. What Is Lightbody? 3rd Edition. Lithia Springs, GA: World Tree. 2007. Print.

Thondup, Tulku. Masters of Meditation and Miracles: Lives of the Great Buddhist Masters of India and Tibet. Boston: Shambhala. 1996. Print.

Walker, DaEl. "The Light Invocation." Crystal Awareness Institute. N.p., 2002. Web. 02 Mar. 2013.

Wilson, Stuart, and Joanna Prentis. The Essenes: Children of the Light. Huntsville, AR: Ozark Mountain. 2005. Print.

About the Author:

Rev. Dr. Cynthia Diane Clayton, often called Karima (her given Sufi name), is a charismatic soul born with great gifts as a SPIRITUAL MEDIATOR and PEACEMAKER. She facilitates harmony between you and your soul, and among all peoples. She finds the common language of love whispered within all hearts.

She is also a trailblazer, blazing new trails in consciousness theory and practices. Although she has a foundation of 40 years in New Thought movement, she is liberated from that box. Her cutting-edge understanding is shared in many circles as the *NEW* thought of New Thought. A guest speaker and workshop facilitator, she speaks at spiritual centers, festivals, universities, and civic organizations.

"She is a treasure trove of spiritual thought and ways to approach life from a position of love and joy. Her eclectic background and degrees give her a much wider per- spective than most speakers, and she's provided a wealth of alternative approaches to spirituality." CSL Board, Clarkston, WA

Receiving a Doctor of Philosophy Degree specializing in Metaphysical Counseling, from the University of Sedona, and a Master of Metaphysical Science, M.Msc. from The University of Metaphysics, her Ph.D., *Separation from Oneness: The Root Cause of Psychological Suffering* holds honors of distinction. Previously she earned a Bachelor of Metaphysical Science, a Bachelor in Sociology, and a Bachelor in Urban & Rural Studies, attending the University of California in San Diego.

"Since the beginning of time I've felt a deep calling to guide and support others." Hence, she created the Inner Energy Matrix©, offering psychological and soul-level healing in her own trade-marked innovative system. She blends Positive Psychology, Transpersonal Psychology, Psychosynthesis, and several supporting healing practices from around the world in a synergy all her own. This is unique counseling which leads clients to their higher power and true Self.

But it wasn't until she became a reverend that her personal Spirit of Guidance truly kicked in as helpmate to humanity. She became an ordained minister with International Metaphysical Ministry, founded by Dr. Paul Leon Masters. Then, she attended training in which she became a "physician of the *heart*," studying sacred texts and practices in all religions and esoteric schools, and received ordination as a Sufi Cheraga (inter-faith minister) by the Sufi Ruhaniyat International. As a minister she performs weddings, house and land blessing ceremonies, and the universal worship service honoring all religions and the divine light existing beyond religion.

Cynthia was recently an adjunct professor at Oregon Coast Community College, offering extremely popular Self-mastery classes she developed from UC Berkeley's Greater Good Science Center and Mindful Schools training.

Practical Metaphysics classes like: "The Science of Happiness," "The Art of Positive Thinking," "Being Happy for No Reason," "Learning to Love Yourself," and "Mindfulness Meditation: Rewire Your Brain for Peace."

"If I were going to say what I consider myself" she confides, "it would be a visionary. It is my strongest trait." She co-produced *An American Visionary*, the film about Barbara Marx-Hubbard, which made its debut in 2017 to a standing ovation at the Illuminate Film Festival. Cynthia Clayton follows in her footsteps as a leader of evolutionary thought, and with similar deep conviction plays a role on the world stage of transformation.

Visit www.cynthiadclayton.com to enjoy her ecstatic poetry fashioned in the style of Rumi, whose birth date she shares, and other inspirations. Order the CD of her spoken word art, *Return to Oneness*. Watch her videos. Or get in contact with her.

CPSIA information can be obtained
at www.ICGtesting.com
Printed in the USA
FFOW02n0355040618
46966572-49229FF